✦ THE ✦
UNICORN
COOKBOOK

ALIX CAREY

summersdale

THE UNICORN COOKBOOK

An Hachette UK Company
www.hachette.co.uk

Summersdale Publishers Ltd
Part of Octopus Publishing Group Limited
Carmelite House
50 Victoria Embankment
LONDON
EC4Y 0DZ
UK

www.summersdale.com

Printed and bound in the Czech Republic

ISBN: 978-1-78685-300-4

Substantial discounts on bulk quantities of Summersdale books are available to corporations, professional associations and other organisations. For details contact general enquiries: telephone: +44 (0) 1243 771107 or email: enquiries@summersdale.com.

For my friends, family, Liam and everyone
who believes in unicorns

ABOUT THE AUTHOR

Alix Carey is a baking enthusiast from Surrey and the author behind food blog and Instagram account My Kitchen Drawer. She is a self-confessed dreamer who wishes on stars and searches for the end of rainbows.

Follow her on Instagram and Twitter **@mykitchendrawer**.

✶ CONTENTS ✶

INTRODUCTION

Did you know that unicorns are a combination of dreams, stardust and sunbeams? Their heads are full of glitter, their hearts are bursting with magic and their eyes shine like stars. Inside this magical book you'll find an array of fun-filled recipes ready to help you unleash your inner unicorn. But before you turn your kitchen into your very own rainbow haven, you need to (figuratively) wear the unicorn cookery badge of honour and the only way to do this is to be given a unicorn name. So, what you waiting for? Go to the facing page, identify your fantasy alter ego and begin your cooking adventure into the world of the most revered mythical creature of all time!

WHAT IS YOUR UNICORN NAME?

To discover your unicorn name, find the initial of your first name and the month you were born in these lists. Combine the two and state your new alias aloud with pride as you don your apron and get ready to create a spread that's out of this world.

A - STARDUST
B - GLITTER
C - SHIMMER
D - GRACEFUL
E - BADASS
F - BUBBLES
G - BRAVE
H - GIDDY
I - MAGIC
J - PIXIE
K - DIAMOND
L - HAPPY
M - ROSY
N - PRINCESS
O - TWIRLY
P - SUNNY
Q - BRIGHT
R - RAINBOW
S - SASSY
T - DARING
U - FIREFLY
V - STARBURST
W - FIERCE
X - MERRY
Y - SPRINKLE
Z - CRAZY

JANUARY - SUNSET STAR
FEBRUARY - TWINKLE TOES
MARCH - CLOUD DREAM
APRIL - FAIRY DUST
MAY - GOLDEN WIND
JUNE - SUGAR PLUM
JULY - SUMMER SHIMMER
AUGUST - FANCY FEET
SEPTEMBER - EMERALD EYES
OCTOBER - SILVER MOON
NOVEMBER - TWILIGHT SHINE
DECEMBER - SPARKLE SOCKS

APRIL X
ELLIe
makenze
bba

CONVERSIONS AND MEASUREMENTS

All the conversions in the tables below are close approximates, which have been rounded up or down. When using a recipe always stick to one measurement; do not alternate between them.

LIQUID MEASUREMENTS

6ml = 1 tsp
15ml = 1 tbsp
30ml = ⅛ cup
60ml = ¼ cup
120ml = ½ cup
240ml = 1 cup
2 tbsp liquid egg white = 1 large egg white

DRIED INGREDIENT MEASUREMENTS

5g = 1 tsp
15g = 1 tbsp
150g flour = 1 cup
225g caster sugar = 1 cup
115g icing sugar = 1 cup
175g brown sugar = 1 cup
200g sprinkles = 1 cup

BUTTER MEASUREMENTS

30g = ⅛ cup
55g = ¼ cup
75g = ⅓ cup
115g = ½ cup
150g = ⅔ cup
170g = ¾ cup
225g = 1 cup

OVEN TEMPERATURES

°C	°F	Gas mark
140	275	1
150	300	2
170	325	3
180	350	4
190	375	5
200	400	6
220	425	7
230	450	8
240	475	9

KITCHEN ESSENTIALS

Before we get started, let's take a look at all the essential ingredients and equipment you'll need.

INGREDIENTS

Butter – Unsalted butter is best for baking and it is easiest to use at room temperature, but when you're making pastry it needs to be cold.

Flour – Most of these recipes call for regular plain flour, but occasionally, when baking cakes, I advise using self-raising flour.

Sugar – The two most important types of sugar for the recipes in this book are caster sugar and icing sugar.

Flavour extracts – A number of recipes in this book require vanilla extract, but there are several others that call for more unusual flavours, such as candy floss and Parma Violet, if you wish to use these.

Eggs – Always use large eggs, unless otherwise specified.

Gel food colouring – These are preferred over liquid food colourings because, most importantly, they do not dilute any mixtures and, secondly, you only need to add a few drops to make rich, vibrant colours.

Sprinkles and pixie dust – You'll have a hard task getting through this book without sprinkles and pixie dust. Many of the recipes here will call for Unicorn Sprinkles (recipe on page 93) so I urge you to make yourself a big batch. The key cake decorations you will need are: hundreds and thousands, chocolate sprinkles, sugar strands, nonpareils (tiny balls made of sugar and starch), edible star- and heart-shaped confetti sprinkles, dragées (edible pearls), sugar crystals and pixie dust (AKA edible glitter).

White chocolate – Whether it be for dipping, coating, drizzling or even baking, white chocolate is a big part of many of these recipes. Of course you are welcome to use dark or milk chocolate as a replacement, but white chocolate adds to the dreamy aura of the unicorn.

EQUIPMENT

Baking trays/tins – You will need at least two flat sheet baking trays, a 27cm x 20cm tray bake tin and a 20cm square brownie tin.

Cake/cupcake tray – All the cakes in this book are baked in 20cm cake tins and you will need at least two (maximum of six). All cupcakes are baked in batches of 12 so you will need a 12-hole cupcake tray as well as a 12-hole mini cupcake tin.

Sugar thermometer – When making confectionery items such as toffee and marshmallow a sugar thermometer will make the recipes failsafe and easier to follow.

Baking paper – The majority of recipes will ask you to line a baking tray or cake tin so baking paper is a necessity. *NOTE: this is not to be confused with greaseproof paper, which is not heat resistant and can cause baked goods to stick to it like glue. Baking paper has a silicon lining and is heat resistant, which prevents any cakes or baked goods from sticking to it.*

Mixing bowls – An assortment of sizes would be ideal, but as long as you have one heatproof mixing bowl you'll get through this book just fine.

Piping bags – Piping bags are used throughout this book for piping buttercream, meringues and batter. You could make your own out of sandwich bags but you'll never achieve the perfectly piped cupcake that way. Piping bags, especially those with a grip, allow you to pipe with absolute accuracy and precision so I would always recommend having a large stash in your kitchen drawer.

Piping nozzles – These come in all shapes and sizes to create a variety of decorations, but I most commonly use the star tips (closed and open) which create decorative swirls and rose patterns and large round tips for macarons, meringue kisses and cake covering.

Cookie cutters – You will find these in a huge variety of shapes and sizes but it's the hearts, rose petals and flowers you'll need for this book. You can purchase packets of these cutters in every size possible from most high-street kitchen retailers.

Rolling pin – A kitchen necessity for bashing biscuits (for a cheesecake base) as well as rolling out pastry and bread.

Cupcake cases – When making cupcakes, you'll need cupcake cases and you can be as adventurous as you wish with the colours. Rainbow and metallic colours are the perfect choice for these recipes.

Electric whisk or standing mixer – While I advocate the use of your own unicorn strength, you'll find an electric whisk or standing mixer much easier and quicker for many of these recipes.

Scales – Baking is a science and requires precise measurements of ingredients.

Measuring spoons – My baking besties. A little lesson to remember: a teaspoon is 5ml and a tablespoon is 15ml. Avoid using normal cutlery to approximate these, as they can range between 2ml and 10ml. This might not sound like much difference, but a sponge cake can crack or sink on as little as a few grams too much or too little baking powder.

Icing smoother – The perfect tool for creating that perfectly smooth buttercream on all your celebration cakes.

Decorating turntable – A 360-degree rotating table makes icing cakes a doddle and allows for easy piping, smoothing and decorating.

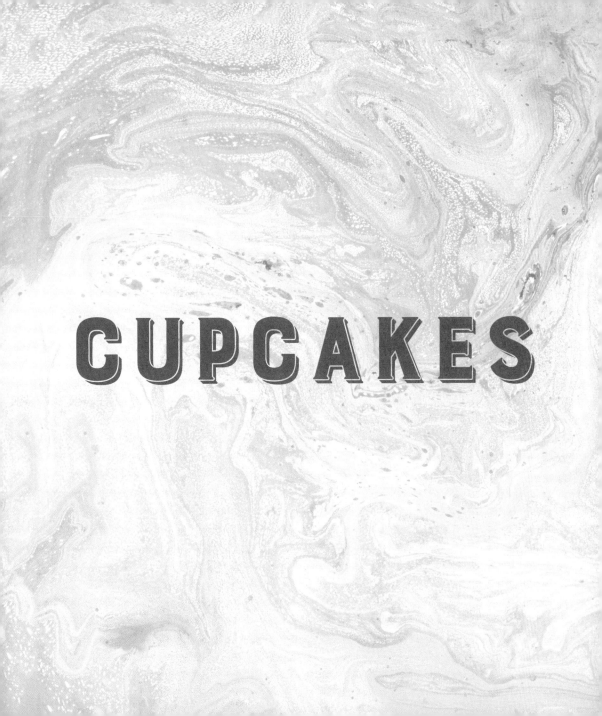

CUPCAKES

⭐ OVER-THE-RAINBOW CUPCAKES ⭐

Take a bite and let these cupcakes take you on a rainbow-filled adventure.

Makes: 12 cupcakes ✷ Time: 1 hour ✷ Difficulty rating: 🌈🌈

INGREDIENTS

For the rainbow sponge:

- ★ 175g butter, softened
- ★ 175g caster sugar
- ★ 175g self-raising flour
- ★ 3 eggs
- ★ 1 tsp lemon zest
- ★ Gel food colouring (pink, blue, purple, yellow and orange)
- ★ Sherbet rainbow belts
- ★ Handful mini marshmallows

For the buttercream:

- ★ 150g butter, softened
- ★ 300g icing sugar
- ★ 1 tsp vanilla extract
- ★ Turquoise gel food colouring

EXTRA EQUIPMENT

You will need a 12-hole cupcake tray, 12 cupcake cases, a piping bag and an open-star piping nozzle.

METHOD

For the cupcakes:

Preheat the oven to 200°C and line a cupcake tray with 12 cupcake cases.

Add the butter, sugar, flour, eggs and lemon zest into a bowl and whisk together for 2–3 minutes until smooth, pale and fluffy.

Split the mixture equally between five bowls and add ¼ tsp of different gel food colouring to each bowl.

Fill the cupcake cases with a teaspoon of each of the coloured batters, place the cupcake tray into the oven and bake for 20 minutes.

Remove from the oven and leave to cool on a wire rack for 20 minutes.

For the buttercream:

Blend the butter and icing sugar together until smooth. Add the vanilla extract and ¼ tsp of gel food colouring and combine.

Transfer the mixture into a piping bag fitted with an open-star nozzle and pipe swirls onto each cupcake.

Cut the sherbet rainbow belts into 5cm strips and position as rainbows on top of the buttercream, with three mini marshmallows at both ends of each rainbow to represent clouds.

15

⋆ STARDUST CUPCAKES ⋆

Did you know that space unicorns live in the Milky Way? As they roam our galaxy they flutter their wings, leaving a trail of silver stardust behind them (some of which you can use to create your own edible universe).

Makes: 12 cupcakes ⋆ Time: 1 hour ⋆ Difficulty rating: ◠◠

INGREDIENTS

For the cupcakes:

- ★ 175g butter, softened
- ★ 175g caster sugar
- ★ 140g self-raising flour
- ★ 50g cocoa powder
- ★ 3 eggs

For the buttercream:

- ★ 150g butter, softened
- ★ 250g icing sugar
- ★ 20g cocoa powder
- ★ Gel food colouring (pink, blue and purple)
- ★ Edible silver glitter
- ★ Silver ball sprinkles

EXTRA EQUIPMENT

You will need a 12-hole cupcake tray, 12 cupcake cases, a piping bag and a closed-star piping nozzle.

METHOD

For the cupcakes:

Preheat the oven to 170ºC and line a cupcake tray with 12 silver cupcake cases.

Place the butter, sugar, flour, eggs and cocoa powder in a bowl and beat together for 2–3 minutes until smooth, pale and fluffy.

Fill each cupcake case with a tablespoon of the silky chocolate batter and bake in the middle of the oven for 20 minutes.

Remove from the oven and leave to cool on a wire rack for 20 minutes.

For the buttercream:

While the cupcakes are cooling, beat together the butter and icing sugar until pale and fluffy.

Split three-quarters of the mixture between three bowls and add ¼ tsp of gel food colouring to each, using a different colour for each bowl.

Add 20g cocoa powder to the remaining quarter of mixture in the main mixing bowl and beat until combined.

To create the galaxy effect, drop teaspoons of each coloured buttercream in any order of your choosing into a piping bag fitted with a closed-star nozzle.

Pipe swirls of buttercream onto each cupcake to reveal the galaxy colours.

Dust each cupcake with a generous coating of edible silver glitter and scatter a few silver ball sprinkles on top.

✷ UNICORN WISH CUPCAKES ✷

If all you wish for is to be a unicorn, then try making these scrummy cupcakes – if you don't start growing a horn or tail, at least you can say you've tasted something out of this world.

Makes: 12 cupcakes ✷ **Time: 1 hour 30 minutes** ✷ **Difficulty rating:** ⌒ ⌒

INGREDIENTS

For the cupcakes:

- ★ 200g butter, softened
- ★ 200g caster sugar
- ★ 200g self-raising flour
- ★ 3 eggs
- ★ Gel food colouring (pink and purple)
- ★ Assorted pink and purple sprinkles
- ★ Edible glitter, silver

For the buttercream:

- ★ 200g butter, softened
- ★ 400g icing sugar

EXTRA EQUIPMENT

You will need a 12-hole cupcake tin, 12 cupcake cases, a cupcake corer or knife, a piping bag and a closed-star piping nozzle.

METHOD

For the cupcakes:

Preheat the oven to 200ºC and line a cupcake tray with 12 cupcake cases.

Add the butter, sugar, flour and eggs into bowl and whisk together for 2–3 minutes until smooth, pale and fluffy.

Split the mixture between two bowls, adding ¼ drop of pink gel food colouring to one and ¼ drop of purple gel food colouring to the other. Try to achieve a pastel tone in each bowl.

Fill each cupcake case with 1 tsp of each coloured batter. Place the cupcake tray into the middle of a preheated oven and bake for 20 minutes.

Remove from the oven and leave to cool on a wire rack for 20 minutes.

Once completely cool use a cupcake corer or knife to remove the centres of each cupcake. Completely fill each centre with an assortment of pink and purple sprinkles then push the cored piece of sponge back into the hole to secure the sprinkles and leave the cupcakes to one side.

For the buttercream:

Whisk together the butter and sugar until pale and fluffy.

Split the mixture equally between two bowls, adding pink food colouring to one bowl and purple food colouring to the other, mixing each until your icing reaches a pastel tone.

Fill two piping bags with the buttercream, one for each colour, then cut the ends and place both into a larger piping bag fitted with a closed-star nozzle.

Pipe swirls of the buttercream onto each cupcake and, finally, scatter with pink and purple sprinkles and a dusting of edible glitter.

✳ MAGICAL UNICORN HORN CUPCAKES ✳

The magical powers of the unicorn horn take this ordinary cupcake and turn it into a glittering rainbow of awesomeness.

Makes: 12 cupcakes ✳ **Time: 1 hour** ✳ **Difficulty rating:** ◠ ◠

INGREDIENTS

For the cupcakes:

* ★ 175g butter, softened
* ★ 175g caster sugar
* ★ 175g self-raising flour
* ★ 3 eggs
* ★ 100g white chocolate chips

For the buttercream:

* ★ 150g butter
* ★ 300g icing sugar
* ★ 1 tsp vanilla extract
* ★ Unicorn Sprinkles (see page 93)

For the unicorn horns:

* ★ 250g white fondant
* ★ 12 cocktail sticks
* ★ Pot of edible glue
* ★ Pot of edible gold paint

EXTRA EQUIPMENT

You will need a 12-hole cupcake tray, 12 cupcake cases, a piping bag, any large tip piping nozzle, two decorating brushes and 12 cocktail sticks.

METHOD

For the cupcakes:

Preheat the oven to 170ºC and line a cupcake tray with 12 silver cupcake cases.

Place the butter, sugar, flour and eggs in a bowl and beat together for 2–3 minutes until smooth, pale and fluffy.

Fold in the white chocolate chips then fill each cupcake case with 1 tbsp of the smooth batter and bake in the middle of the oven for 20 minutes.

Remove from the oven and leave to cool on a wire rack for 20 minutes.

For the unicorn horns:

While the cupcakes are cooling you can begin making your unicorn horns.

Insert a cocktail stick into a sturdy fruit or vegetable, such as an orange or a potato, leaving the tip of the stick to be the size you want your horn to be.

Take a small ball of fondant (around the size of a ping-pong ball) and roll it out into a tapered rope shape.

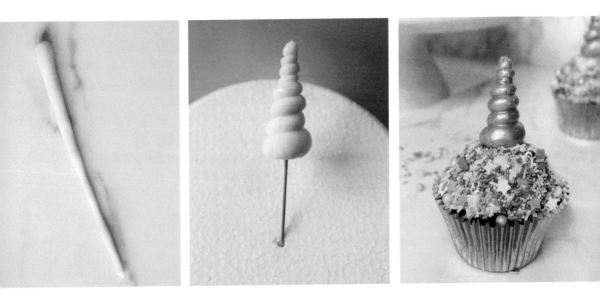

Using a small decorating brush, coat the cocktail stick in edible glue, then twist the tapered fondant around the cocktail stick until you reach the top. Leave the glue to set for 2–3 minutes.

Paint the horn gold with your edible paint and the second paintbrush, then leave it all to dry while you ice the cupcakes.

For the buttercream:

Cream together the butter, icing sugar and vanilla extract until smooth and fluffy.

Transfer the buttercream into a piping bag, fitted with any large nozzle of your choosing, and pipe it onto the cupcake making sure the surface is fully coated – don't worry too much about the swirl being perfect.

Assembling the unicorn horn cupcake:

Pour the Unicorn Sprinkles into a shallow bowl, then pick up your buttercream-topped cupcakes and one by one gently dip them into the bowl of sprinkles. Carefully tilt the cake to ensure all sides are well coated, then lift and fill in any gaps by hand.

Take your dry unicorn horns and stick them onto the centre of each cupcake.

Serve with a dusting of magic.

✳ COLOUR-ME CUPCAKES ✳

Although the unicorn is synonymous with sparkles and magic, it began its humbler days as a horse. Just like the evolution of this majestic beast, the first step to creating these gorgeous cupcakes is to whip up some light, unassuming sponges.

Makes: 12 cupcakes ✳ **Time: 1 hour** ✳ **Difficulty rating:** ◠ ◠

INGREDIENTS

★ 175g butter, softened

★ 175g caster sugar

★ 175g self-raising flour

★ 3 eggs

★ Zest of 1 lemon

EXTRA EQUIPMENT

You will need a 12-hole cupcake tray and 12 cupcake cases.

METHOD

Preheat the oven to 200°C and line a cupcake tray with 12 cupcake cases.

Place the butter, sugar, flour, eggs and lemon zest into a bowl and whisk together for 2–3 minutes until smooth, pale and fluffy.

Fill each cupcake case with the lemon batter and place the cupcake tray into the middle of a preheated oven and bake for 20 minutes.

Remove from the oven and leave to cool for 20 minutes.

Once fully cooled, pipe with swirls of Colour-Me Buttercream (see page 25).

✳ COLOUR-ME BUTTERCREAM ✳

Silky to taste, marvellous to look at – you'll want to top all of your food creations with this crazily colourful Swiss meringue buttercream.

Makes: enough to pipe 12 cupcakes ✳ Time: 45 minutes ✳
Difficulty rating: ◠◠

INGREDIENTS

- ★ 3 egg whites
- ★ 250g caster sugar
- ★ 300g butter, softened and cut into small chunks
- ★ Gel food colouring (pink, blue, yellow and orange)

EXTRA EQUIPMENT

You will need a piping bag and a closed-star piping nozzle.

METHOD

Place the egg whites and sugar in a bowl over a pan of simmering water and stir until the sugar dissolves.

Remove from the heat and whisk the mixture until it becomes thick. Add the chunks of butter and whisk the mixture at high speed until you have a fluffy buttercream.

Split the mixture equally between four bowls and add ¼ tsp of different gel food colouring to each bowl so you have four vibrant bowls of buttercream. Fill four piping bags with each of the colours then lay out a sheet of cling film.

Pipe a line of the yellow buttercream onto the cling film, followed by the orange, pink and blue, then roll it together into a sausage, twisting the ends of the cling film to secure.

Cut one end and transfer the cling film roll into a piping bag fitted with a closed-star nozzle, then pipe rainbow swirls of the mixture onto each cupcake.

ABCDE FGHIJ K Q V S T Y W Q S

AMRQ

CELEBRATION CAKES

✶ RAINBOW CAKE ✶

This impressive rainbow cake may require lots of time, patience and oven space to complete, but it provides quite a showstopper for any party. (Even the mighty unicorn would be tempted to stop and stare at its magnificence.)

Makes: 1 cake ✶ Time: 2 hours ✶ Difficulty rating: ⌒ ⌒

INGREDIENTS

For the sponge:

* ★ 500g self-raising flour
* ★ 500g butter, softened
* ★ 500g caster sugar
* ★ 6 eggs
* ★ 1 tsp baking powder
* ★ 1 tsp vanilla extract
* ★ Gel food colouring (pink, blue, green, yellow, orange and red)

For the buttercream:

* ★ 400g butter, softened
* ★ 800g icing sugar

To decorate:

* ★ Smarties

EXTRA EQUIPMENT

You will need three or six 20cm cake tins, a 25cm diameter cake board and a palette knife.

METHOD

For the sponge:

Preheat the oven to 180°C and line the 20cm cake tins with baking paper. I recommend baking this cake in batches so you can fit it all in the oven.

Add half the butter, sugar, flour, eggs, baking powder and vanilla into a bowl and mix together until smooth, pale and fluffy.

Split the mixture equally between three bowls and add ¼ tsp of different gel food colouring to each bowl (pink, blue and green) until you have three batches of vibrant cake batter.

Fill three cake tins with each coloured batter, making sure they are level, then place the tins into the pre-heated oven and bake for 20 minutes or until you can insert a skewer into the sponge and it comes out clean.

Remove from the oven and leave to cool in the tins for 15 minutes before lifting out and placing on a wire rack to cool completely.

Repeat the above with the remaining half of the ingredients, this time colouring the bowls yellow, orange and red.

For the buttercream:

Combine the butter and icing sugar and mix until smooth, pale and fluffy.

Assembling the cake:

Layer the cake together by adding a little buttercream to a 25cm cake board and sticking the pink sponge on top. Add 1 tbsp of buttercream to the top of the pink sponge and spread it out across the entire surface, then add the blue sponge. Avoid cross-contamination of crumbs by decanting the buttercream into five separate bowls and cleaning the palette knife after each layer of buttercream.

Continue with the green sponge, followed by the yellow, orange and red. Then begin covering the entire cake with a thin layer of buttercream and smooth it out with a palette knife.

Leave in the fridge for an hour until the buttercream has hardened, then bring the cake back out and cover with a thicker layer of buttercream, smoothing it out with a palette knife.

To decorate:

Add a circle of purple Smarties to the outside edge of the top of the cake, followed by green, yellow, orange and red.

✴ MAGICAL EXPLOSION CAKE ✴

When a unicorn can't contain its happiness any longer, it bursts into the mother of all magical cakes. It'll certainly leave a lasting impression on the special people lucky enough to eat it.

Makes: 1 cake ✴ Time: 5–6 hours (in stages) ✴
Difficulty rating: ◗ ◗ ◗

INGREDIENTS

For the sponge:
* 500g self-raising flour
* 500g butter, softened
* 500g caster sugar
* 6 eggs
* 1 tsp baking powder
* 1 tsp vanilla extract
* Gel food colouring (pink, orange, yellow, green, blue and purple)

For the ombre rainbow buttercream:
* 500g butter, softened
* 1kg icing sugar
* 4 tbsp milk
* Gel food colouring (pink, yellow, orange, blue and purple)

To decorate:
* 200g dark chocolate
* Unicorn Sprinkles (see page 93)
* Unicorn Rocks (see page 67)
* Unicorn Kisses (see page 72)
* Smarties

EXTRA EQUIPMENT

You will need three or six 20cm cake tins, a 25cm diameter cake board, a palette knife, an icing smoother and a decorating turntable.

METHOD

For the sponge:

I recommend baking this cake in batches so you can fit it all in the oven. The following instructions will guide you to bake this in two batches. However, if you have enough oven space and six cake tins then please proceed and make it all in one go using all the sponge ingredients together.

Preheat the oven to 180°C and line three 20cm cake tins with baking paper.

Add half the butter, sugar, flour, baking powder, eggs and vanilla into a bowl and beat together for 2–3 minutes until smooth, pale and fluffy.

Split the mixture equally between three bowls and add 1–2 drops of a different gel food colouring (pink, orange and yellow) to each so you have three bowls of pastel cake batter.

Pour each mixture into a separate cake tin, place all tins into the preheated oven and bake for 20 minutes.

Remove from the oven and leave to cool in the tins for 15 minutes before lifting out and placing on a wire rack to cool completely.

Repeat the above with the remaining half of the ingredients, this time colouring the cake batter green, blue and purple.

For the ombre rainbow buttercream:

For your base layer of buttercream, combine 250g butter and 500g icing sugar, and blend in a stand mixer or with a handheld whisk for 4 minutes until smooth, pale and fluffy. Then add 2 tbsp milk and mix it in so it is easier to coat the cake.

For the rainbow buttercream, combine the remaining 250g butter and 500g icing sugar and, again, blend in a stand mixer or with a handheld whisk for 4 minutes until smooth, pale and fluffy. Then add 2 tbsp milk and mix again. Split the mixture between five bowls and add 1–2 drops of gel food colouring to each bowl (pink, yellow, orange, blue and purple) until you have five bowls of pastel buttercream.

Fill five piping bags, one piping bag per colour and leave to one side.

Assembling the cake:

Layer the cake together by adding a little of the base buttercream to the 25cm cake board so that your first sponge layer (purple) can be 'glued' to the base. Add a tablespoon of the base buttercream to the top of the purple sponge and spread it out across the entire surface, then add the blue sponge.

Continue with the green sponge, followed by the yellow, orange and pink, then begin covering the entire cake with a thin layer of buttercream and smooth it out with a palette knife.

Leave in the fridge for an hour or overnight to allow the buttercream to harden.

To create the ombre effect:

Sit your cake on an icing turntable, take the piping bag with your purple buttercream and, starting at the bottom, pipe two rings of icing around the cake, spinning the turntable as you pipe. Then take your piping bag with the blue buttercream and pipe another two rings around the cake. Continue piping rings with the orange, yellow and pink buttercream until you reach the top of the cake. *NB: This step does not have to look perfect. You do not need to use lots of icing for this, but enough so that when you smooth it out, there will be no cake showing through.*

Once all the colours have been applied, begin blending the buttercream colours together using a palette knife starting from the bottom up. Remove any excess buttercream from the palette knife as you blend all the buttercream together but do not worry about making things perfect just yet.

Once all the colours have been blended together with a palette knife, it's time to smooth them together using an icing smoother. For best results, place the icing smoother edge lightly on the cake, with the bottom touching the turntable, and rotate the cake around, continuing until the surface is smooth. If you need to go around the cake again, clean your icing smoother and repeat.

Put the cake back into the fridge to cool for 30 minutes in preparation for the final stage – the chocolate drip.

For the chocolate drip:

Break the chocolate into squares and place in a heatproof bowl over a pan of simmering water to melt gently.

Take the cooled cake out of the fridge and place it back onto the turntable. Using a tablespoon, spoon the melted chocolate onto the centre of the cake, then using the back of the spoon spread the chocolate around the top of the cake till it reaches the edges.

Slowly push a bit of the chocolate over the edge with the back of the spoon so it drips down the sides and continue to do this all the way around. It looks nicer when drips aren't uniform so you can push a bit more and a bit less as you go along.

Sprinkle the edges of the cake with some Unicorn Sprinkles, then decorate it with Unicorn Rocks exploding from the centre and Unicorn Kisses positioned on top and some down the sides of the cake. Finally, adorn the cake with a selection of Smarties and a final dusting of sprinkles.

⭐ UNICORN KISSES CAKE ⭐

Only very special people receive unicorn kisses and this cake has one on each slice ready to sweep you off your feet.

Makes: 1 cake ✳ Time: 2–3 hours ✳ Difficulty rating: 🌙🌙

INGREDIENTS

For the sponge:

- ★ 300g self-raising flour
- ★ 300g butter, softened
- ★ 300g caster sugar
- ★ 4 eggs
- ★ 1 tsp baking powder
- ★ 1 tsp vanilla extract

For the buttercream:

- ★ 400g butter, softened
- ★ 800g icing sugar
- ★ 3 tbsp milk
- ★ Blue gel food colouring

To decorate:

- ★ Unicorn Kisses (see page 72)
- ★ Pink pearl sprinkles

EXTRA EQUIPMENT

You will need three 20cm cake tins, a 25cm diameter cake board, a palette knife, an icing smoother and a decorating turntable.

METHOD

For the sponge:

Preheat the oven to 180°C and line three 20cm cake tins with baking paper.

Place the butter, sugar, flour, baking powder, eggs and vanilla into a bowl and beat together for 2–3 minutes until smooth, pale and fluffy, then fill the three cake tins with the batter and bake for 20 minutes.

Remove from the oven and leave to cool in the tins for 15 minutes before lifting out and placing on a wire rack to cool completely.

For the blue buttercream:

Beat the butter and icing sugar in a bowl for 4 minutes until smooth, pale and fluffy. Then add 2 tbsp milk and a drop of blue gel food colouring and mix it through thoroughly until well combined.

Assembling the cake:

Add a little buttercream to the 25cm cake board so that your first sponge layer can be secured to the base. Continue sandwiching the remaining sponge layers one by one with a generous portion of buttercream in between each layer.

Cover the entire cake with a thin layer of buttercream and smooth it out with a palette knife. Leave in the fridge for an hour or overnight if you have time, to allow the buttercream to harden.

Add a second, thicker coat of buttercream using a palette knife to smooth it around, then take your icing smoother and place it lightly on the cake, with the bottom touching the turntable, and rotate the cake around. If you need to go around the cake again, clean your icing smoother and repeat.

Take a handful of sprinkles and gently press them against the bottom half of the cake, continuing until you have coated the cake as required.

Top with seven Unicorn Kisses, one for each portion of cake, and serve.

✷ SWEET DREAMS CAKE ✷

One taste of this cake and you're guaranteed sweet dreams.

Makes: 1 cake ✷ Time: 2–3 hours ✷ Difficulty rating: ◠◠

INGREDIENTS

For the ombre sponge:

- ★ 400g self-raising flour
- ★ 400g butter, softened
- ★ 400g caster sugar
- ★ 6 eggs
- ★ 1 tsp baking powder
- ★ 1 tsp vanilla extract
- ★ Pink gel food colouring

For the Swiss meringue buttercream:

- ★ 3 egg whites
- ★ 250g caster sugar
- ★ 300g butter, softened and cut into small chunks

To decorate:

- ★ Pink and white pearl sprinkles

EXTRA EQUIPMENT

You will need four 20cm cake tins, a 25cm diameter cake board, a palette knife, an icing smoother and a decorating turntable.

METHOD

For the ombre sponge:

Preheat the oven to 180°C and line four 20cm cake tins with baking paper.

Place the butter, sugar, flour, baking powder, eggs and vanilla into a bowl and whisk together for 2–3 minutes until smooth, pale and fluffy.

Divide the mixture equally between four bowls and add a tiny drop of pink gel food colouring to each to create a pale pink tone. Put one bowl to the side and add a second drop of pink food colouring to one of the remaining bowls, mixing it in so it is a shade darker than the pale pink bowl, then put it to one side so you are left with two bowls. Continue with the final two bowls until you have four bowls of cake batter in different shades of pink.

Transfer each shade of cake batter into a separate cake tin and bake for 20 minutes.

Remove from the oven and leave to cool in the tins for 15 minutes before lifting out and placing on a wire rack to cool completely.

For the Swiss meringue buttercream:

Place the egg whites and sugar in a heatproof bowl over a pan of simmering water and stir slowly but continuously until the sugar dissolves.

Remove from the heat and whisk the mixture until it thickens, then add the chunks of softened butter and whisk the mixture at high speed until you have a fluffy, silky buttercream.

Assembling the cake:

Add a little buttercream to the 25cm cake board so that your first sponge layer (the darkest pink one) can be secured to the base. Continue sandwiching the remaining sponge layers, dark to light, with a generous portion of buttercream in between each layer.

Cover the entire cake with a thin layer of buttercream and smooth it out with a palette knife, then leave in the fridge for an hour to harden.

Add a second, thicker coat of buttercream, using a palette knife to smooth it around, then take your icing smoother and place it lightly on the cake, with the bottom touching the turntable, and rotate the cake. If you need to go around the cake again, clean your icing smoother and repeat.

Take a handful of sprinkles, scatter them across the top of the cake and serve.

✷ MAJESTIC UNICORN CAKE ✷

Transform any ordinary cake into a unicorn with these edible fondant decorations.

Makes: decorations for 1 cake ✷ Time: 1 hour ✷ Difficulty rating: ◠◠

INGREDIENTS

For the horn and the ears:

* ★ 250g caramel fondant icing
* ★ 250g white fondant icing
* ★ Edible gold paint
* ★ Edible gold glitter

For the eyes:

* ★ 50g black fondant icing

For the hair:

* ★ 200g butter, softened
* ★ 400g icing sugar
* ★ Pink gel food colouring

EXTRA EQUIPMENT

You will need two decorating brushes, one 9cm bamboo skewer, three to four small piping bags, an open-star piping nozzle, a round tip nozzle, a rolling pin, and large and small rose petal-shaped cutters.

METHOD

For the basic cake recipe:

The cake sponge and buttercream colours are optional and you can be as creative as you wish. However, for a basic vanilla cake and buttercream please see the Unicorn Kisses Cake on page 34 for a vanilla cake recipe and the Sweet Dreams Cake on page 36 for the Swiss meringue buttercream coating.

For the horn:

You'll need to prop up your bamboo skewer so that you have both hands available to work with the fondant icing. The best way to do this is to wedge the stick in an egg-sized ball of spare fondant icing, leaving enough length to create your horn.

Making sure you have plenty of worktop space, take a large ball of caramel fondant (around the size of a tennis ball) and roll it out into a tapered strip where one end is slightly thicker than the other.

Coat the bamboo skewer in edible glue with a decorating brush, then twist the tapered fondant around the stick, starting from the thicker end until you reach the top. Leave the glue to set for 2–3 minutes.

Paint the horn gold with the edible paint using the second paintbrush, dust over a little gold glitter and put it to one side to dry.

Once dry, carefully place it onto the centre of the cake.

For the ears:

Roll out some white fondant and caramel fondant and cut two large ear shapes from the white fondant using a large rose petal cutter, then cut two smaller petal shapes from the caramel fondant, using the small rose petal cutter.

Stick the caramel petal on top of the white petal using a little water to bond both pieces, then use the tip of a butter knife to indent the centres of the ears. Paint the two smaller petal shapes with the gold paint, pinch the bases of each of the petal shapes together slightly to create an ear shape and leave to set. Prop them up in an empty egg carton to help keep their shape.

For the eyes:

For the eyes, roll out two thin strips of black fondant. Pinch each one in half and taper the ends to form V shapes. Set aside to firm up a little before adding to your cake.

For the hair:

In a large bowl or standing mixer, whisk together the softened butter and icing sugar until pale and fluffy. Split the mixture into three bowls and colour them different shades of pink using drops of the pink gel food colouring.

Fit a piping bag with a closed star piping nozzle and fill it with the darkest pink colour. Pipe swirls of buttercream onto the cake, starting from the centre and in line with the horn. Continue piping a few small and large swirls across the top and down one side of the cake to create a 'mane' of buttercream unicorn hair, leaving space to pipe other swirls in the lighter shades of buttercream.

Fit another piping bag with a closed nozzle and fill it with a lighter shade of pink. Pipe peaks of buttercream over the cake in the gaps of the buttercream mane.

Continue with the final piping bag and pink mixture, adding swirls and peaks of buttercream until the mane is complete.

Complete the look by placing the ears either side of the horn, using a swirl of buttercream to prop them up.

COOKIES
AND
BISCUITS

✷ PINK VELVET COOKIES ✷

Everything a unicorn loves turns pink and these cookies are no exception. Studded with white chocolate, marshmallows and heart sprinkles, what's not to love?

Makes: 12 cookies ✶ **Time: 45 minutes** ✶ **Difficulty rating:** ◠ ◠

INGREDIENTS

* 100g butter
* 75g golden caster sugar
* 1 egg
* Pink gel food colouring
* 175g self-raising flour
* 100g white chocolate chips
* 50g mini marshmallows
* Heart sprinkles
* 2 tbsp milk

METHOD

Preheat oven to 170°C and line two baking trays with baking paper.

Beat the butter and sugar until light and fluffy, then add the egg and ¼ tsp pink gel food colouring and mix well.

Sift in the flour and add the milk, chocolate chips, marshmallows and sprinkles, then fold together.

Place spoonfuls of the mixture onto the prepared trays, leaving enough space around each as the mixture will spread when cooking, and place in the oven for around 8–10 minutes.

Remove from oven and place on a wire rack to cool.

These will keep for 2–3 days in an airtight container.

✸ MAKE-A-WISH SHORTBREADS ✸

These melt-in-the-mouth biscuits are so moreish that you'll be making unlimited amounts to keep your unicorn friends happy! (Don't forget to make a wish when you take a bite into the middle of them.)

Makes: 12 biscuits ✶ **Time: 1 hour** ✶ **Difficulty rating:** ◠ ◠

INGREDIENTS

★ 225g butter, softened

★ 65g icing sugar

★ 1 tsp vanilla extract

★ 1 egg

★ ¼ tsp salt

★ 160g plain flour

★ 100g strawberry jam

★ Unicorn Sprinkles (see page 93)

EXTRA EQUIPMENT

You will need a rolling pin, a 10cm heart-shaped cutter and an 8cm heart-shaped cutter.

METHOD

Preheat oven to 180ºC and line two baking trays with baking paper.

Cream together the butter and icing sugar until smooth and fluffy, then add the egg and vanilla and beat together, making sure all the ingredients are combined.

Sift the flour and fold into the mixture gradually to form a dough.

Create a ball shape with the dough, cut in half and roll into two separate balls. Wrap each ball of dough in cling film and place in the fridge to firm for 10 minutes.

Roll out each ball on a floured surface to a thickness of approximately 5mm and, using a 10cm heart-shaped cutter, prepare 12 heart shapes from each ball of dough and, using the 8cm heart-shaped cutter, cut out 12 smaller hearts in the centre of each 10cm heart, removing the scraps from the centre. You should have 24 heart shapes in total. (You can roll out the scraps and make some mini heart biscuits to minimise waste.)

Using a palette knife, carefully transfer each heart shape to your pre-prepared baking trays, leaving a 5cm space between each one in case the mixture spreads during cooking. Pop the trays into the fridge for 10 minutes.

Once the dough is firm, remove the trays from the fridge and place in the preheated oven to bake for 8 minutes until the edges begin to brown. Remove each shortbread from the baking tray and leave to cool on a wire rack.

Once cool, sprinkle the top biscuits with icing sugar and set aside. Add a teaspoon-sized dollop of jam to the centre of the base biscuits, spreading a little towards the edges but ensuring the jam stays in the centre. Place the icing sugar-dusted biscuits on top of the jam-covered biscuits and fill the centres with Unicorn Sprinkles.

Eat immediately if you must, but these will keep in an airtight container for 2–3 days.

✶ GINGERBREAD GEMS ✶

The perfect treat when you need a small dose of rainbow-coloured happiness.

Makes: 24 biscuits ✳ **Time: 2 hours** ✳ **Difficulty rating:** 🌙🌙

INGREDIENTS

For the biscuits:

- ★ 75g butter
- ★ 3 tbsp golden syrup
- ★ 60g light brown sugar
- ★ 175g plain flour
- ★ ¼ tsp bicarbonate of soda
- ★ 2 tsp ground ginger

For the topping:

- ★ 150g royal icing
- ★ 25ml cool water
- ★ Gel food colouring (pink, blue, green and yellow)

EXTRA EQUIPMENT

You will need a 3cm flower-shaped cutter, piping bags and a closed-star piping nozzle.

METHOD

Preheat the oven to 180ºC and line a baking tray with baking paper.

Place the butter, golden syrup and light brown sugar into a pan and stir on a low heat until the sugar has dissolved. Remove from the heat and leave to cool for 10 minutes.

Sift together the flour, bicarbonate of soda and ginger in a mixing bowl, make a well in the centre, and pour in the sugar and butter mixture.

Mix together to form a dough and create a ball shape using your hands. Wrap the dough in cling film and place in the fridge to firm for 30 minutes.

Lay the chilled dough between two sheets of floured baking paper and use a rolling pin to roll out to a thickness of approximately 5mm.

Remove the top layer of baking paper then cut out 25 shapes using the flower-shaped cutter. Remove the scraps and transfer the flower biscuits to the lined baking tray. Bake for 10–12 minutes until golden.

Remove from the oven and transfer to a wire rack to cool.

While they're cooling whisk together the royal icing and water until the mixture holds stiff peaks and is firm enough to pipe.

Split the mixture between four bowls and add a different coloured drop of gel food colouring to each, stirring it in.

Fit a closed-star nozzle to four small piping bags and fill each bag with a different coloured icing mixture. Pipe a little icing onto each biscuit, lifting the piping bag up sharply to create the peak effect.

Leave the royal icing to set hard for an hour then serve. These will keep in an airtight container for 2 days.

⋆ HUG-ME COOKIE CUPS ⋆

Unicorns give the best hugs and, while you may never experience one for real, these cookie cups are the closest you'll get.

Makes: 20 cookies ⋆ **Time: 1 hour** ⋆ **Difficulty rating:** ◠ ◠

INGREDIENTS

For the cookie cups:

- ★ 160g flour
- ★ 1 tsp cornflour
- ★ 1 tsp baking powder
- ★ ¼ tsp salt
- ★ 60g butter, softened
- ★ 40ml vegetable oil
- ★ 85g caster sugar
- ★ 1 egg
- ★ 1 tsp vanilla extract
- ★ 100g multi-coloured sugar strand sprinkles

For the ganache topping:

- ★ 120g white chocolate
- ★ 65ml double cream
- ★ 50g multi-coloured sugar strand sprinkles

EXTRA EQUIPMENT

You will need a 12-hole mini cupcake tin, a piping bag and a closed-star piping nozzle.

METHOD

For the cookie cups:

Preheat oven to 170°C and grease a mini cupcake tin.

Sift together the flour, cornflour, baking powder and salt in a bowl.

In a separate, large bowl, cream together the butter, oil and sugar until smooth.

Add the egg and vanilla extract then slowly fold in the flour until the mixture comes together as a dough.

Add the sprinkles and mix in by hand.

Take 1 tsp of mixture and roll it into a ball that fills the mini cupcake hole. Do this for each mini cupcake.

Using a spoon, press down into each ball to create a well centre then pop the mini cupcake tray into the fridge for 20 minutes to firm up.

Bake for 10 minutes, and then remove and immediately recreate the well in the centre with the back of a spoon and leave them to cool and firm while you make the ganache topping.

For the ganache topping:

Break the white chocolate into squares and place in a heatproof bowl over a pan of simmering water. Add the double cream and let the two melt together, stirring occasionally.

Once all has melted remove from the heat and refrigerate for 20 minutes until firm.

Fill a piping bag fitted with a closed-star nozzle with the ganache and pipe into the cookie wells followed by a generous scattering of multi-coloured sugar strand sprinkles.

These will keep for 3–4 days in an airtight container.

✷ FUNFETTI BISCOTTI ✷

Anything double-baked sounds daunting, but get this biscotti recipe right and you'll level up to a promising pastry chef.

Makes: 20 biscotti ✳ **Time: 2 hours** ✳ **Difficulty rating:** ◠◠

INGREDIENTS

- ★ 250g flour
- ★ ½ tsp baking powder
- ★ 250g caster sugar
- ★ 3 eggs, beaten
- ★ 100g white chocolate chips
- ★ 200g multi-coloured sugar strand sprinkles
- ★ 100g white chocolate

METHOD

Preheat the oven to 160°C and line a large baking tray with baking paper.

Mix together the flour, baking powder and sugar in a bowl, and add the beaten eggs slowly to make a dough.

Pour the mixture out onto a floured surface and knead in the chocolate chips and half the multi-coloured sugar strand sprinkles gently. Separate and roll into two logs, then place them 5cm apart on the lined baking tray and bake for 25 minutes.

Remove from the oven, let cool for 10 minutes and reduce the oven temperature to 140°C.

Once slightly cooled, cut the logs into 1–2cm thick slices and lay them out on the baking tray.

Return the biscotti to the oven and bake for 10–15 minutes, then turn over and continue to bake for another 10–15 minutes until golden-brown. The idea behind this double baking is that the end result is a hard biscuit.

Transfer the biscotti to a wire rack and leave to cool for 15–30 minutes.

Meanwhile, break the white chocolate into squares and place in a heatproof bowl over a pan of simmering water.

Once the chocolate has melted, dip one side of the biscotti into it and scatter multi-coloured sugar strand sprinkles over the top so they stick to the chocolate. Do this with the remaining biscotti and return to the wire rack to allow the chocolate to set.

✳ FABULOUSLY FRUITY TARTS ✳

Savour these delicious, tangy flavours on a balmy evening and be transported into your very own Midsummer Night's Dream.

Makes: 8–10 tarts ✳ **Time: 2 hours** ✳ **Difficulty rating:** ◠◠

INGREDIENTS

- ★ 300g plain flour
- ★ 150g cold butter, cubed
- ★ 2 tbsp cold water
- ★ 1 egg
- ★ Fruit jam
- ★ 100g icing sugar
- ★ Pink gel food colouring
- ★ Multi-coloured sugar strand sprinkles to decorate

EXTRA EQUIPMENT

You will need a rolling pin.

METHOD

Preheat the oven to 200°C and line two baking trays with baking paper.

In a large bowl combine the flour and cold butter with your fingertips until the mixture resembles fine breadcrumbs.

Add the cold water 1 tbsp at a time and bring the dough together.

Knead the dough into a ball and wrap in cling film, then leave in the fridge for 30 minutes to chill.

Roll out into a 40cm x 80cm rectangle and with a pizza cutter or knife cut out 6cm x 10cm rectangles – you will need two rectangles per tart.

Lay out pairs of pastry squares onto the baking trays and create an egg wash by combining a beaten egg and 1 tbsp of water. Using a pastry brush, dab egg wash along the edges of one of the rectangles.

Scoop 1 tsp of fruit jam into the centre of each rectangle, being careful not to overfill or you will have a jam explosion. Top with the second piece and crimp the edges with a fork to seal them together. Prick the centre with a fork to allow steam to release when baking and give them a final brush of egg wash.

Bake for 20–25 minutes until golden brown, then leave to cool on a wire rack.

Once completely cool, mix together the icing sugar, water and ¼ tsp pink gel food colouring until you have a thick consistency. Spoon onto the tops of the pastry and, of course, cover in multi-coloured sugar strand sprinkles.

Leave for 30 minutes to allow the icing to set before eating.

You can plan ahead and make these raw and freeze them, so they are ready to bake and decorate when needed.

✷ MAGIC MATCHSTICKS ✷

Strike while hot and you may even be able to make sparks fly.

Makes: 24 sticks ✷ **Time: 1 hour 20 minutes** ✷ **Difficulty rating:** ◠

INGREDIENTS

For the biscuits:

- ★ 250g butter, softened
- ★ 65g icing sugar
- ★ 1 tsp vanilla paste
- ★ 250g plain flour
- ★ 1 tsp cornflour

For the topping:

- ★ 500g white chocolate
- ★ Gel food colouring (purple, pink and blue)
- ★ 4 tbsp hundreds and thousands

EXTRA EQUIPMENT

You will need a rolling pin.

METHOD

For the biscuits:

Preheat the oven to 180°C and cover two baking trays with baking paper.

Cream together the butter and sugar until fluffy and stir in the vanilla paste.

Fold in the flour and cornflour gradually until the mixture comes together as a dough and shape it into a ball with your hands. Wrap the ball in cling film and place into the fridge to firm for 30 minutes.

Roll the dough out between two sheets of floured baking paper to approximately 2cm thickness, then remove the top baking paper and cut into 24 10cm stick shapes.

Transfer the dough sticks to a baking tray and bake for 15–20 minutes until the edges begin to brown.

Remove from the oven and cool on a wire rack for 20–30 minutes until firm.

For the topping:

Break the white chocolate into squares and place in a heatproof bowl over a pan of simmering water to melt.

Split the melted white chocolate between three bowls and stir ¼ tsp of different gel food colouring into each to give a pastel tone.

Split the shortbread sticks into three groups, ready to dip into the separate bowls of coloured chocolate. Once half of each stick is coated, lay them on a wire rack and sprinkle hundreds and thousands over the chocolate before it cools.

Leave to set for 30 minutes before tucking in.

These will keep in an airtight container for 2–3 days.

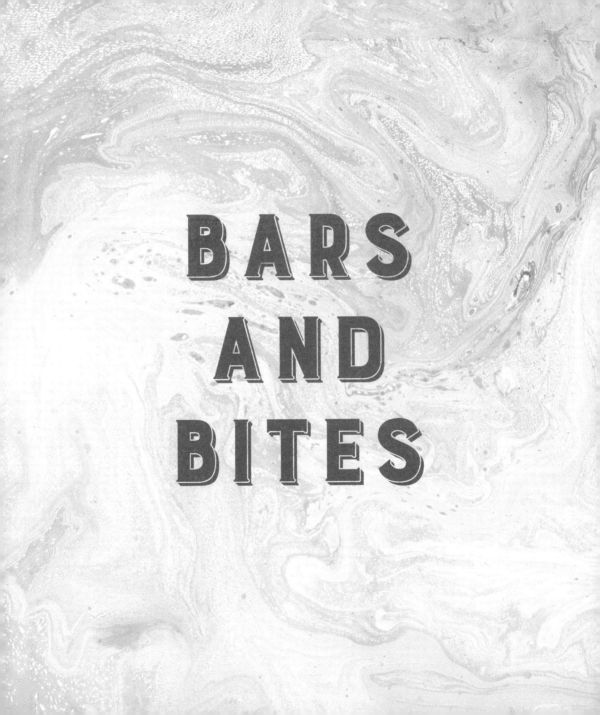

BARS AND BITES

★ PINKIE BARS ★

These sweet treats are the perfect size to have as an afternoon snack – but as they are moreishly good one is often never enough!

Makes: 9 bars ✶ Time: 1 hour 30 minutes ✶ Difficulty rating: ◠◠

INGREDIENTS

- ★ 200g salted butter, cubed
- ★ 250g white chocolate, broken up
- ★ Pink gel food colouring
- ★ 300g caster sugar
- ★ 4 eggs
- ★ 120g self-raising flour
- ★ 150g white chocolate chips
- ★ 100g dried cranberries

EXTRA EQUIPMENT

You will need a 20cm square cake tin and a large metal spoon.

METHOD

Preheat your oven to 160ºC and line a 20cm square cake tin.

Melt the chocolate and butter in a heatproof bowl over a pan of simmering water. Once the ingredients have melted, add 2–3 drops of pink food colouring and mix together, then leave to one side to cool slightly.

While the mixture cools, whisk the sugar, three eggs and then separate the fourth egg and add just the egg yolk in a large bowl until well combined. Add this to the melted chocolate and butter mixture and whisk the two mixtures together for around 1 minute.

Add the flour, white chocolate chips and cranberries, and carefully fold the mixture together using a large metal spoon.

Spoon the pink batter into the prepared cake tin and smooth it out until level. Bake for 40 minutes, but check after 30 minutes and if the surface is browning too much cover it with some foil.

Remove from the oven, leave in the tin and set aside to cool completely before peeling off the baking paper and cutting into squares.

✶ RAINBOW CHEESECAKE BROWNIES ✶

Full of unicorn secrets and dreams, these brownies are the ultimate sweet treat.

Makes: 16 brownies ✶ Time: 1 hour ✶ Difficulty rating: ⌒⌒

INGREDIENTS

For the brownies:

- ★ 225g dark chocolate (minimum 70% cocoa)
- ★ 150g unsalted butter
- ★ 3 eggs
- ★ 225g caster sugar
- ★ 100g plain flour

For the cheesecake:

- ★ 150g cream cheese
- ★ 50g caster sugar
- ★ 1 egg
- ★ Gel food colouring (pink, blue, yellow, orange)

EXTRA EQUIPMENT

You will need a 20cm square baking tin.

METHOD

For the brownie batter:

Preheat oven to 170ºC, and grease and line a 20cm square baking tin.

Melt the chocolate and butter in a heatproof bowl set over a pan of simmering water. Once the ingredients have melted, remove the bowl from the pan and set aside to cool slightly.

While the mixture cools, whisk the eggs and caster sugar in a large bowl until well combined. Add the eggs and sugar to the melted chocolate and butter and mix for around 1 minute.

Add the flour and carefully fold it into the mixture using a metal spoon until fully incorporated.

For the cheesecake mixture:

Beat the cream cheese, caster sugar and egg together until smooth.

Split the mixture between four bowls and add ¼ tsp of different gel food colouring to each bowl.

Spoon the brownie mixture into the cake tin and smooth it into all the corners. Spoon the cheesecake mixtures in a random formation on top. Using a knife, swirl the two mixtures together to give a rainbow marble effect.

Bake in the oven for 25–30 minutes. Remove from oven, leave in the tin and set aside to cool completely before peeling off the baking paper and cutting into squares.

Hepping tade for mum?

✮ INTERGALACTIC TOFFEE ✮

Transport your tastebuds to infinity and beyond with these Parma Violet-infused toffee sweets topped with swirls of edible glitter and sprinkles.

Makes: 24 pieces ✶ Time: 3 hours 30 minutes ✶ Difficulty rating: 🌙🌙

INGREDIENTS

- ★ 397g condensed milk (this might seem an odd amount but it's the volume of a standard tin)
- ★ 140g soft light brown sugar
- ★ 80g butter
- ★ Parma Violet food flavouring
- ★ Purple gel food colouring
- ★ Pink and purple sprinkles, stars and edible glitter to decorate

EXTRA EQUIPMENT

You will need a square baking tin and a sugar thermometer (optional).

METHOD

Line a square tin with baking paper and leave to one side.

Place the condensed milk, sugar and butter in a large pan and melt the ingredients together on a low heat.

Once all the sugar has fully dissolved and the butter has melted bring the mixture to a boil, stirring continuously until it reaches 113°C. This is known as the 'soft ball' stage.

Use a sugar thermometer, or you can test it after 5 minutes by dropping a small piece of the mixture into a glass of cold water. If it forms a soft flexible ball that flattens like a pancake in your hand then it is ready.

Turn off the heat and add 2–3 drops of Parma Violet flavouring and 2–3 drops of purple gel food colouring, mixing them together until fully incorporated. Keep stirring for 8 minutes until the mixture begins to thicken, then transfer to your prepared tin and smooth out evenly.

Sprinkle over a generous layer of pink and purple sprinkles, stars and edible glitter, then leave to set for 2–3 hours.

Once firm, remove from the tin and measure out into 4cm x 4cm squares. To make the cutting easier dip a sharp knife into boiling water before cutting the squares.

These will keep in an airtight container for 1 week.

✴ DAZZLING DOUGHNUTS ✴

At night, the unicorn is a magnificent sight to behold. These dazzling doughnuts are as deep and velvety as the sky it roams.

Makes: 6 doughnuts ✴ Time: 45 minutes ✴ Difficulty rating: ◠ ◠

INGREDIENTS

For the doughnuts:

- ★ 100g self-raising flour
- ★ 30g cocoa powder
- ★ 1 tsp baking powder
- ★ 100g caster sugar
- ★ 200ml milk
- ★ 2 eggs
- ★ 50g butter
- ★ 1 tsp vanilla extract
- ★ Purple gel food colouring

For the glaze:

- ★ 100ml double cream
- ★ 125g icing sugar
- ★ Gel food colouring (blue, purple and pink)

EXTRA EQUIPMENT

You will need a six-hole doughnut tin.

METHOD

To make the doughnuts:

Preheat oven to 180ºC, and spray a doughnut tin with a good dose of non-stick cooking spray and set aside.

In a large bowl, whisk together half the flour and half the baking powder with the cocoa powder, then in another bowl mix the remaining flour and baking powder together.

In a separate bowl, mix together the sugar, eggs, butter, vanilla and milk, and beat together until well combined.

Make a well in the chocolate dry mix and pour half the wet ingredients into it, mixing them together until just combined. Pour the remaining wet mixture into the second dry mix bowl with a drop of purple gel food colouring and mix them together until just combined.

Spoon the purple batter into half of the doughnut cavities and the chocolate batter into the other half, making sure to only fill them about two-thirds to three-quarters of the way full.

Bake for 8–10 minutes or until a toothpick inserted into the doughnut comes out clean.

Remove from the oven and allow to cool for about 5 minutes in the tin. Remove the doughnuts from the tin and transfer to a wire rack to cool.

To make the glaze:

In a separate bowl, mix together the double cream and icing sugar. If the glaze is too thick, slowly add 1 tsp more double cream at a time until it has reached your desired consistency.

Split the mixture between three bowls and, using ¼ tsp of gel food colouring for each, colour one bowl blue, the other purple and the last pink until you reach your desired colour tone.

Spoon the three different coloured mixtures into another clean bowl and swirl them together to create a marble effect.

Dip the tops of the doughnuts into the glaze and transfer back to the wire rack to cool and allow the glaze to harden. Top with sprinkles or glitter.

✭ UNICORN ROCKS ✭

A unicorn's sparkle never goes unnoticed and these shards of unicorn rock are no exception.

Makes: 1 slab ✶ Time: 1 hour 15 minutes ✶ Difficulty rating: 🌈

INGREDIENTS

★ 400g white chocolate

★ Gel food colouring (pink, purple and turquoise)

★ Unicorn Sprinkles (see page 93)

★ Edible glitter

EXTRA EQUIPMENT

You will need a cocktail stick.

METHOD

Line a baking tray with baking paper and set aside.

Place the squares of white chocolate in a heatproof bowl over a pan of simmering water and, stirring occasionally, let it melt down completely.

Remove from the heat and split the white chocolate equally between three bowls.

Add a ¼ tsp different gel food colouring to each bowl and then place spoonfuls of each mixture in a random formation onto the baking paper. Swirl the mixture together gently with a cocktail stick and scatter sprinkles and edible glitter over the top.

Leave to set at room temperature for 1 hour then break into shards and enjoy.

✷ MYSTICAL MARSHMALLOWS ✷

The puff of the powder as you bite into these marshmallows reflects
the beautiful mystery of the unicorn.

Makes: 20–30 squares   ✷   Time: 2–3 hours   ✷   Difficulty rating: ◗ ◗ ◗

INGREDIENTS

- ★ 50g icing sugar
- ★ 50g cornflour
- ★ 14g powdered gelatine
- ★ 275ml water
- ★ 450g caster sugar
- ★ 2 tsp vanilla extract
- ★ Gel food colouring (pink, blue, yellow and purple)

EXTRA EQUIPMENT

You will need a 20cm square tin and a sugar thermometer.

METHOD

This recipe is complex and requires you to act fast, so you will need to ensure you have all ingredients weighed out and equipment prepared in advance.

Before you begin cooking, lay out four bowls and four teaspoons. Grease a 20cm square tin with sunflower oil, line the tin with baking parchment and grease the paper with the remaining oil. Mix together the icing sugar and cornflour, and dust the tin with a little of the mixture to evenly coat the base and sides. Reserve the remaining icing sugar and cornflour mixture for later.

When you're ready, place the gelatine and 100ml of the cold water into a mixing bowl and set aside for 10 minutes to soften. Once softened, you'll need to blend the mixture using a stand mixer or handheld whisk on its lowest setting.

Pour the sugar and the remaining 175ml of cold water into a saucepan and bring to a rolling boil on a medium heat, stirring until the sugar dissolves.

Reduce the heat and simmer the mixture until it reaches a temperature of 113°C (use a sugar thermometer to gain the exact temperature).

As soon as the sugar syrup reaches the correct temperature, take the pan off the heat and gradually pour the syrup into the blended gelatine/water mix, being extra cautious as the mixture will be extremely hot.

Whisk slowly and continuously until all of the mixture has been fully incorporated into the syrup.

Add the vanilla extract, then whisk for another 5–7 minutes at a faster speed.

Once the mixture has been thoroughly whisked, divide it equally between the four bowls you laid out earlier and colour each bowl with a ¼ tsp different gel food colouring.

Spoon the coloured mixtures into the tin and run a cocktail stick or knife through them to create a mystical swirly effect.

Dust the top of the marshmallow with a little more of the icing sugar and cornflour mixture, then cover the tin with cling film and store in a cool, dry place for 1–2 hours, or overnight, to set. *NB: do not chill in the fridge.*

Once the marshmallow mixture has set, turn it out onto a clean work surface dusted with the remaining icing sugar and cornflour mixture. Peel off the parchment paper and cut the marshmallow into cubes.

Store in an airtight container in a cool, dry place for up to 3 weeks.

✸ UNICORN COOKIE DOUGH BITES ✸

If cookie dough on its own isn't enough to make one drool, try this recipe for ultimate cookie dough delight.

Makes: 40 bites ✶ Time: 1 hour 30 minutes ✶ Difficulty rating: ◖◗

INGREDIENTS

For the cookie dough:

- ★ 100g soft brown sugar
- ★ 100g butter, softened
- ★ 125g plain flour
- ★ 200g condensed milk
- ★ 1 tbsp vanilla extract
- ★ 100g dark chocolate chips
- ★ 100g multi-coloured sugar strand sprinkles
- ★ Unicorn Sprinkles (see page 93)

For the ganache topping:

- ★ 150g white chocolate
- ★ 120ml double cream
- ★ 100g icing sugar
- ★ Turquoise gel food colouring

EXTRA EQUIPMENT

You will need a piping bag and a round-tipped piping nozzle.

METHOD

For the cookie dough:

Line a rectangular baking tray with baking paper.

Combine the sugar and butter in a large bowl until evenly blended. Add the flour, condensed milk and vanilla, and mix until you have a thick dough, then fold in the chocolate chips and sprinkles.

Spread the dough out into the baking tin, pressing it down firmly into one even layer, then chill in the fridge for 1 hour.

For the ganache topping:

While the dough is chilling, place the white chocolate and double cream into a saucepan and simmer over a low to medium heat. Stir frequently until fully melted and then add 1 drop of the turquoise gel food colouring to create a pale green tone.

Take off the heat and leave to cool for 10 minutes, then mix in the icing sugar. The consistency of the ganache should end up being firm enough for you to be able to pipe.

Transfer the mixture to a piping bag fitted with a round nozzle, then remove the chilled cookie dough from the fridge and top it with peaked piped rounds of ganache.

Add Unicorn Sprinkles to decorate and slice into bite-sized chunks.

✶ UNICORN KISSES ✶

The sweetest kiss of all is one from a unicorn and these colourful peaks of meringue are the next best thing.

Makes: 35 kisses ✶ Time: 1 hour 30 minutes ✶ Difficulty rating: ◠◠◠

INGREDIENTS

- ★ 75g caster sugar
- ★ 75g icing sugar
- ★ 3 egg whites
- ★ Gel food colouring (pink, yellow and purple)

EXTRA EQUIPMENT

You will need three piping bags, a round piping nozzle, a closed-star piping nozzle and three paintbrushes.

METHOD

Preheat the oven to 120°C and line two large baking trays with baking paper.

In a small bowl, mix both of the sugars together and set aside.

In a clean bowl, whisk the egg whites on a medium speed for 2 minutes until they form stiff peaks.

Begin adding the sugar a tablespoon at a time, whisking for 30 seconds between each tablespoon. Continue until you have used all the sugar and have a glossy meringue that holds stiff peaks.

Turn a piping bag inside out and paint three lines of the pink gel food colouring with a paintbrush from the top to almost the end of the bag. Turn the piping bag back the right way so the painted lines are on the inside and fit it with a round piping nozzle.

Fill with a few tablespoons of the meringue mix and twist the end to close. Holding the bag at a 90-degree angle over one of the lined trays, apply pressure at the start, then quickly draw the bag upwards to create little points. The colour will give the meringues the stripy pattern as they pass through the bag.

Repeat with another piping bag, this time painting it yellow.

Split the remaining meringue mixture into two bowls, colouring one bowl pale pink and the other pale purple. Fit two piping bags with closed star nozzles and fill them with the coloured meringue mixture, one colour in each piping bag. Holding the bag at a 90-degree angle over the second lined tray, apply pressure at the start, then quickly draw the bag upwards to create little points.

Bake in the oven for 1 hour or until they sound hollow when tapped. Leave to cool in the oven, then store in a plastic food bag or airtight container until ready to use.

PARTY
FOOD

✦ FAIRY DUST MACARONS ✦

*Did you know that fairies are a unicorn's best friend? All you need
is faith, trust and a little magic dust.*

Makes: 12 macarons ✶ Time: 2 hours ✶ Difficulty rating: ◠ ◠ ◠

INGREDIENTS

For the meringue shells:

- ★ 70g ground almonds
- ★ 140g icing sugar
- ★ 2 large egg whites,
  room temperature
- ★ 50g caster sugar
- ★ Gel food colouring
  (pink and purple)
- ★ Unicorn Sprinkles
  (see page 93)

For the buttercream:

- ★ 100g butter, softened
- ★ 200g icing sugar
- ★ Pink gel food colouring
  and candy floss flavouring
- ★ Unicorn sprinkles
- ★ Edible glitter

EXTRA EQUIPMENT

You will need piping bags and a round-tip nozzle.

METHOD

For the meringue shells:

Preheat the oven to 140–150°C and prepare two baking trays
with baking paper and leave to one side.

Place the ground almonds and icing sugar in a food processor,
blitz for about a minute and transfer to a mixing bowl.

Beat one of the egg whites into the almond and icing sugar mix to
make a smooth paste. Split the paste equally between two bowls
and add a drop of pink gel food colouring to one and a drop of
purple gel food colouring to the other.

Stir the colour into the paste, then cover with a tea towel.

Pour the second egg white into a super-clean bowl and begin to
whisk. Gradually add the caster sugar, 1 tbsp at a time, until it
starts to stiffen. Beat on a high setting for the final 2 minutes until
the mixture resembles stiff, glossy peaks.

Divide your fluffy egg whites evenly between your pink and purple
almond paste mixtures, then using a spatula slowly fold the egg
white and paste together from the bottom up. Continue this
motion around 15–20 times until the mixture is fully incorporated
and flows like molten lava. This is what we call 'macaronage'.

Transfer the macaronage into two piping bags and cut the ends.

Place both piping bags into a larger bag fitted with a 1cm nozzle and pipe 24 rounds of the mixture at a 90-degree angle onto the two lined baking trays. The mixture will spread so only pipe half the size you wish the end macaron to be (roughly 2cm wide).

Sprinkle each round with Unicorn Sprinkles, tap the trays on the work surface to remove any air bubbles, then leave them to dry for 30 minutes. They will be ready to bake when they are no longer sticky or wet when touched.

Bake on the middle shelf of the oven for 8 minutes. Open the oven to let out any steam and turn the trays around, then bake for a further 8 minutes until the tops are crisp. Leave them to cool fully before removing from the baking sheet.

For the buttercream:

Cream together the butter and icing sugar until smooth and fluffy.

Add a drop of pink gel food colouring and 2–3 drops of candy floss flavouring, followed by the sprinkles and edible glitter then fold together.

Transfer to a piping bag fitted with a small star nozzle then pipe swirls of buttercream onto half of the macaron shells. Top with the remaining macarons and leave in the fridge for 30 minutes before enjoying.

These will store in an airtight container for a few days if kept in the fridge.

★ END-OF-THE-RAINBOW MACARONS ★

You might not find a pot of gold at the end of these rainbows, but you will be joyously satisfied when you taste the flavours of these scrummy macarons.

Makes: 12 macarons ✳ **Time: 2 hours** ✳ **Difficulty rating:** ◖◖◖

INGREDIENTS

For the meringue shells:

★ 70g ground almonds
★ 140g icing sugar
★ 2 large egg whites, room temperature
★ 50g caster sugar
★ Blue gel food colouring

For the buttercream:

★ 100g butter, softened
★ 200g icing sugar
★ Vanilla extract

To decorate:

★ Sherbet rainbow belts

EXTRA EQUIPMENT

You will need a piping bag and a round-tipped piping nozzle.

METHOD

For the meringue shells:

Preheat the oven to 140–150°C and prepare two baking trays with baking paper and leave to one side.

Place the ground almonds and icing sugar in a food processor, blitz for about a minute and transfer to a mixing bowl.

Beat one of the egg whites into the almond and icing sugar mix to make a smooth paste. Add a drop of blue gel food colouring then stir through until combined and set aside.

Pour the second egg white into a super-clean bowl and begin to whisk. Gradually add the caster sugar, 1 tbsp at a time, until it starts to stiffen, then beat on a high setting for the final 2 minutes until the mixture resembles stiff, glossy peaks.

Add the egg whites to your blue almond paste mixture, then slowly fold the egg white and paste together using a spatula from the bottom up. Continue this motion around 35–40 times until the mixture is fully incorporated and flows like molten lava. This is what we call 'macaronage'.

Transfer the macaronage into a piping bag fitted with a 1cm nozzle. For each macaron shell, pipe three small rounds of mixture at a 90-degree angle to form a cloud/triangle shape. The mixture will spread so only pipe half the size you wish the end

macaron to be (roughly 2cm wide). Repeat this process until you have 24 cloud/triangle shapes.

Tap the trays on the work surface to remove any air bubbles, then leave them to dry for 30 minutes. They will be ready to bake when they are no longer sticky or wet when touched.

Bake on the middle shelf for 8 minutes. Open the oven to let out any steam, turn the trays around and bake for a further 8 minutes until the tops are crisp. Leave them to cool fully before removing from the baking sheet.

For the buttercream:

Cream together the butter and icing sugar until smooth and fluffy. Add a drop of vanilla extract and fold together.

Transfer to a piping bag fitted with a small flower nozzle and pipe swirls of buttercream onto half of the macaron shells. Top with the remaining macarons and pipe a little buttercream onto each end of the top shells.

To decorate:

Cut the rainbow ribbons to 5cm strips and position as a rainbow on top of the buttercream. Leave in the fridge for 30 minutes before enjoying.

These will keep in an airtight container in the fridge for a few days.

✦ DIY CAKE POPS ✦

Take your unicorn creativity to new heights with these bite-sized balls of rainbow happiness.

Makes: 20 cake pops ✦ Time: 1–2 hours ✦ Difficulty rating: 🌈

INGREDIENTS

For the sponge:
* 120g butter, softened
* 150g caster sugar
* 1 tsp vanilla extract
* 2 eggs
* 180g self-raising flour
* 4 tbsp milk

For the frosting:
* 80g butter, softened
* 40g cream cheese, softened
* 1 tsp vanilla extract
* 200g icing sugar, sifted

For the decoration:
* 500g melted white chocolate
* 1 tsp vegetable oil
* Gel food colouring (pink, purple, green, yellow, orange and blue)
* Assortment of sprinkles (see page 9)

EXTRA EQUIPMENT

You will need lollipop sticks and a cake-pop stand.

METHOD

For the sponge:

Preheat the oven to 180°C and line a 20cm cake tin and baking tray with baking paper.

Place the butter, sugar, flour, milk, eggs and vanilla into a bowl and beat together for 2–3 minutes until smooth, pale and fluffy.

Pour the mixture into the pre-prepared tin, bake for 35–40 minutes and leave the cake to cool on a wire rack.

For the vanilla cream cheese frosting:

Cream the butter, vanilla and cream cheese together until smooth and gradually add the sugar, then continue to mix until light and fluffy. Refrigerate for 30 minutes before using.

For the cake pops:

Crumble the cooled sponge in a large mixing bowl with your hands until you have fine crumbs.

Add heaped tablespoons of the cream cheese frosting and begin mixing it in with the crumbs. You may not require all the frosting as it will depend how moist your sponge is. Keep mixing and adding frosting until you have a fudge-like texture that doesn't crumble when squeezed between your hands.

Wrap the mixture in cling film and chill for at least 1 hour to firm up.

Once chilled, break off small pieces of the mixture (about the size of a ping-pong ball) and roll them into balls with your hands. Place each ball on the lined baking tray and put in the fridge for 15–20 minutes.

For the decoration:

Meanwhile, lay out some bowls of your selected sprinkles for decoration and put to one side.

Melt the white chocolate in a heatproof bowl set over a pan of simmering water then mix in 1 tsp of vegetable oil. This will make the melted chocolate smoother and easier to coat the cake pop. Divide it equally between six bowls, adding a few drops of different gel food colouring to each bowl.

Take the cake balls out of the fridge and divide into six groups of four – one for each bowl of colour. For each colour group, dip a lollipop stick a quarter of the way into the coloured melted chocolate, then push it halfway into the cake balls. Dipping the stick into the chocolate first helps to keep it attached to the cake ball. Dip each ball into the coloured chocolate ensuring it is fully coated.

Decorate with your selected sprinkles, as elaborately as you wish, place into the cake pop stand and chill in the fridge or in a cool room for 1 hour before serving.

✳ SPARKLING UNICONES ✳

It's a well-known fact that the unicorn's horn is the source of all its magical powers. Create some magic of your own by making these edible, glittering beacons of happiness.

Makes: 6 horns ✳ **Time: 30 minutes, plus drying time** ✳
Difficulty rating: 🌈

INGREDIENTS

- ★ 200g white chocolate
- ★ 6 waffle ice cream cones
- ★ Champagne sugar crystals
- ★ Edible gold paint

EXTRA EQUIPMENT

You will need a new paintbrush.

METHOD

Line a baking tray with baking paper and set aside.

Place the white chocolate squares in a heatproof bowl over a pan of simmering water, stirring occasionally until it melts down completely.

Pour the melted chocolate into a mug and dunk each cone, with the tip facing downwards, into the mug until it's completely coated.

Stand the cones on the pre-prepared baking tray, scatter generously with sugar crystals and leave to allow the chocolate to set.

When completely set, take a clean paintbrush (one that is new or has only been used in baking before) and paint the wider end of the cone with the gold paint.

Leave to dry before eating. You can use these for ice creams, fill them with sponge cake or sweets or simply eat them as they are. The creative possibilities are limitless.

✶ UNICORN DIP ✶

Take your favourite biscuit and dip into some magic – the fluffiest cheesecake mix that will make you believe in unicorns.

Makes: 1 bowl to serve 6 ✶ Time: 20 minutes ✶
Difficulty rating: ◠

INGREDIENTS

- ★ 250g cream cheese
- ★ 250g marshmallow fluff
- ★ 100g icing sugar
- ★ 1 tsp vanilla
- ★ 120ml double cream
- ★ Gel food colouring (pink, purple, yellow, blue)
- ★ Unicorn Sprinkles (see page 93)
- ★ Biscuits, for serving such as butter biscuits or cookies

METHOD

Combine the cream cheese, marshmallow fluff and icing sugar in a large bowl and beat with a hand whisk or standing mixer until evenly combined. Add the double cream and vanilla and continue beating until smooth and fluffy.

Divide the mixture equally between four bowls and add a couple of drops of different gel food colouring to each bowl to create pastel tones.

Add spoonfuls of the coloured mixture into a serving bowl, alternating colours until you've used up all the mixture. Swirl the colours together with a palette knife or cocktail stick, then top with Unicorn Sprinkles.

Serve with your favourite biscuits.

✶ RAINBOW JELLY ✶

This layered rainbow jelly is an instant party crowd-pleaser. It may be time-consuming but it's well worth the perseverance.

Makes: 4 jellies ✶ Time: 5–6 hours ✶ Difficulty rating: 🌈

INGREDIENTS

- ★ 60g blackcurrant jelly
- ★ 60g lime jelly
- ★ 60g orange jelly
- ★ 60g raspberry jelly
- ★ 60g strawberry Jelly
- ★ 700ml boiling water, divided by 5 (140ml per jelly layer)
- ★ 700ml cold water, divided by 5 (140ml per jelly layer)

EXTRA EQUIPMENT

You will need four clear 250ml dessert dishes or glasses.

METHOD

Break apart the blackcurrant jelly cubes and put them into a mixing bowl.

Measure out 140ml boiling water and pour it over the cubes, stirring continuously until they completely dissolve.

Measure out 140ml cold water and add this to the dissolved jelly, then stir everything together.

Pour the mixture into a measuring jug so it's easier to pour and divide the mixture out between four clear serving dishes – you'll need them to be clear so all the layers are visible.

NB: you may not need to use all the mixture, as you need to ensure there is an equal amount of room for all the other jelly layers in the serving dish/glass. How much you use will depend on the volume of your dish/glass, but this recipe makes four 250ml glasses.

Leave to cool and set in the fridge for approximately 1 hour.

Repeat this method with the lime, orange, raspberry and strawberry jellies until you have filled your glasses to the rim.

Serve as is or with some whipped cream.

✦ UNICORN POPCORN ✦

Plain popcorn is an acceptable treat in the mortal world, but if you want to ascend to the mythical realms, you need to give your popcorn some pizazz.

Serves: 2 ✳ Time: 30 minutes ✳ Difficulty rating: ⌒

INGREDIENTS

- 300g cooked popcorn
- 150g pink and white marshmallows
- 100g white chocolate
- Turquoise gel food colouring
- Unicorn Sprinkles (see page 93)

METHOD

Add the marshmallows to a heatproof bowl and set over a pan of simmering water.

Stir occasionally until the marshmallows have melted and remove the bowl from the heat. Pour in 200g popcorn and a handful of Unicorn Sprinkles and mix until all popcorn is roughly coated.

In another heatproof bowl, melt the white chocolate over a pan of simmering water then remove the bowl from the heat, add a small drop of turquoise gel food colouring and mix it in.

Add the remaining 100g popcorn and another handful of Unicorn Sprinkles and mix it around until all are roughly coated.

Leave the two to set and then once hard break into small popcorn pieces and serve.

✷ STRAWBERRY ICE LOLLIES ✷

Be as cool as a unicorn with these tasty summer treats.

Makes: 4 lollies   ✶   Time: 20 minutes, plus freezing overnight   ✶
Difficulty rating: ◠

INGREDIENTS

For the lollies:

- ★ 200g fresh strawberries, chopped
- ★ 2 tbsp sugar
- ★ 200ml Greek yoghurt
- ★ 100ml water

EXTRA EQUIPMENT

You will need a four-hole ice-lolly mould and four lolly sticks.

METHOD

In a bowl mix the chopped strawberries and sugar together and mash with a fork.

Add the Greek yoghurt and water and mix together to combine.

Transfer the mixture to a measuring jug and pour it into the lolly moulds. Place the lolly sticks in halfway.

Place in the freezer to set for 2–3 hours or overnight.

To remove the lollies from the mould, run them under a tap of hot water for 3 minutes then carefully pull on the sticks to release them. Be patient and gentle to avoid breaking the lolly.

✷ UNICORN SPRINKLES ✷

Get creative and bring some unicorn magic to your baking every day with these DIY Unicorn Sprinkles.

Makes: 200g sprinkles ✶ Time: 15 minutes ✶ Difficulty rating: 🌈

INGREDIENTS

* ★ 40g hundreds and thousands
* ★ 40g edible star- and heart-shaped confetti sprinkles
* ★ 30g pink and purple nonpareils (tiny balls)
* ★ 30g dragées (silver balls)
* ★ 30g dragées (pearl balls)
* ★ 30g edible gold confetti

EXTRA EQUIPMENT

You will need an airtight container.

METHOD

Add each type of sprinkle into a large bowl and combine them well.

Using a teaspoon, spoon the mixture into an airtight container and give it a little shake.

Use these marvellous sprinkles to add some magic to any sweet treats, adding instant sparkle and glitz.

These will keep in an airtight container for at least 3 years.

BREAKFAST

✸ HAPPINESS PANCAKES ✸

Sprinkle some happiness over breakfast and wake up smiling with these rainbow pancakes.

Makes: 12 pancakes ✶ Time: 30 minutes ✶ Difficulty rating: ⌒

INGREDIENTS

For the pancakes:

- ★ 150g plain flour
- ★ ½ tsp salt
- ★ 1 tbsp baking powder
- ★ 1 tsp caster sugar
- ★ 225ml milk
- ★ 1 egg
- ★ 1 tsp butter or oil for frying
- ★ Gel food colouring (purple, pink, blue, green, yellow, orange)

For the toppings:

- ★ Squeeze of honey
- ★ Unicorn Sprinkles (see page 93)
- ★ Mini marshmallows

METHOD

Sift together the flour, salt, baking powder and sugar in a large bowl. Make a well in the centre, pour in the milk, then add the egg and whisk until the pancake batter is smooth.

Divide the mixture between six bowls and add ¼ tsp of different gel food colourings (purple, pink, blue, green, yellow and orange) to each.

You will be frying the pancakes colour by colour so start by pouring the purple batter into a measuring jug.

Heat a frying pan over a medium heat and lightly grease it with a knob of butter. When the butter has melted and started to bubble pour two rounds of the pancake batter into the pan.

Cook each pancake until bubbles appear on the surface, then flip with a spatula and cook for 30 seconds on the reverse side. You don't want to brown them too much or you'll lose the colour. Set aside the cooked pancakes on a plate and put into your oven, set to 100°C, to keep them warm.

Continue with the remaining colours of batter, cleaning the measuring jug in between each. Serve hot with a squeeze of honey, a dash of Unicorn Sprinkles and marshmallows.

✳ MAGICAL SMOOTHIE BOWL ✳

Unleash your inner unicorn every morning with this delicious, magical bowl of healthy goodness.

Makes: 1 bowl ✳ Time: 30 minutes ✳ Difficulty rating: 〜

INGREDIENTS

For the raspberry smoothie:

- ★ 1 banana
- ★ 100g frozen raspberries
- ★ 50g frozen beetroot
- ★ 100ml yoghurt
- ★ Handful of ice

For the blueberry smoothie:

- ★ 1 banana
- ★ 100g frozen blueberries
- ★ 100ml yoghurt
- ★ Handful of ice

To decorate:

- ★ 4 strawberries, halved
- ★ 1 banana, sliced
- ★ Handful of frozen blueberries
- ★ 3 tbsp desiccated coconut
- ★ Squeeze of lemon juice

EXTRA EQUIPMENT

You will need a blender and a 1cm heart cutter.

METHOD

For the fruit:

Slice one of your bananas and cut out heart shapes from each slice using your 1cm heart cutter. Then slice your strawberries thinly. Squeeze a little bit of lemon juice over the fruit to keep it from turning brown and put them both to one side.

For the raspberry smoothie:

Put 1 banana, the raspberries, beetroot, yoghurt and ice into a blender and blitz until smooth. It will take a few pulses for everything to combine and it will feel like it needs more liquid at first but try not to add any more as you want it to be a thick consistency. Pour into a jug and leave in the fridge while you make the blueberry smoothie.

For the blueberry smoothie:

Put 1 banana, the frozen blueberries, yoghurt and ice into a clean blender and blitz until smooth as above.

Transfer the raspberry smoothie into a bowl, then on one side pour the blueberry smoothie so you have half and half.

Lay your heart shaped banana slices on the blueberry side, followed by the strawberry slices. Add a handful of blueberries on the raspberry side and finally a generous scattering of desiccated coconut.

✶ DREAMS ON TOAST ✶

Turn your toast into a triumph and begin your mornings with a burst of colour with this fun yet nourishing recipe.

Makes: 2 slices ✶ Time: 15 minutes ✶ Difficulty rating: ◠

INGREDIENTS

- ★ 2 slices of white bread, toasted
- ★ 250g cream cheese
- ★ Gel food colouring (yellow, pink, green and blue)
- ★ 1 avocado
- ★ 6 strawberries

EXTRA EQUIPMENT

You will need a 1cm star cutter.

METHOD

Split the cream cheese mixture between four bowls and add a drop of different gel food colouring (yellow, pink, green and blue) to each to create a pastel tone.

Toast two slices of white bread in a toaster or under a grill and then leave to cool slightly.

Halve an avocado and cut the strawberries into thick slices. Using a 1cm star cutter, cut out star shapes from each and leave to one side.

With a butter knife, add the cream cheese to the toasted bread at a diagonal angle, starting with the yellow, followed by pink, green and blue.

Add the strawberry and avocado toppings and serve immediately.

�֎ RAINBOW SWIRL BREAD ✦

Unicorns eat rainbows for breakfast, lunch and dinner.
With this rainbow swirl bread, you can too.

Makes: 1 loaf ✦ Time: 2–3 hours ✦ Difficulty rating: ⌒⌒⌒

INGREDIENTS

* ★ 230ml milk
* ★ 1 egg yolk
* ★ 1 tbsp butter, melted
* ★ 7g active dry yeast
* ★ 350g white bread flour
* ★ 30g granulated sugar
* ★ 7g salt
* ★ Gel food colouring (pink, yellow, green, blue and purple)

EXTRA EQUIPMENT

You will need a 23cm x 13cm loaf tin.

METHOD

Combine the milk and egg yolk in a non-stick saucepan and simmer on a low heat for 1 minute, until the mixture is warm to touch, lightly whisking the ingredients all the while.

Add the melted butter and yeast to the warm mixture then set aside.

Combine the flour, sugar and salt in a large bowl and pour in the milk mixture, stirring together until it forms a rough dough.

Tip the dough onto a lightly floured surface and knead it together for roughly 10 minutes until it comes together and is smooth and elastic.

Divide the dough into six equal pieces and place each piece in a separate small bowl, covering each with a tea towel so they don't start to dry.

Begin colouring each dough by placing a piece on a cutting board (or any surface you're willing to cover with food colouring). Add a few drops of one gel food colouring and knead it into the dough (using gloves to prevent tie-dye hands). Add more colouring to make brighter, if necessary.

Place the coloured ball into a small bowl, cover with cling film and place in a warm spot to 'prove' for an hour or until it has doubled in size.

Repeat with the remaining pieces of dough, dying each a different colour and ensuring you wash your hands and work surface in between each colour to prevent them mixing.

When all the pieces of dough have doubled in size, remove the pink dough and roll it out on a lightly floured surface into a 20cm x 10cm rectangle. Roll out the yellow piece of dough into a 20cm x 10cm rectangle and place it directly on top of the pink dough. Repeat with the green, then blue, then purple dough until you have a stack of five 20cm x 10cm rectangles.

Roll up the dough from the shortest end and place into a lightly greased 23cm x 13cm loaf tin.

Cover with a tea towel and prove once more for an hour or until it has doubled in size.

Preheat the oven to 180°C, uncover the dough and bake for 30 minutes, until lightly browned on top.

Remove from the loaf tin and let it cool completely on a wire rack before slicing and unveiling the beautiful rainbow swirls.

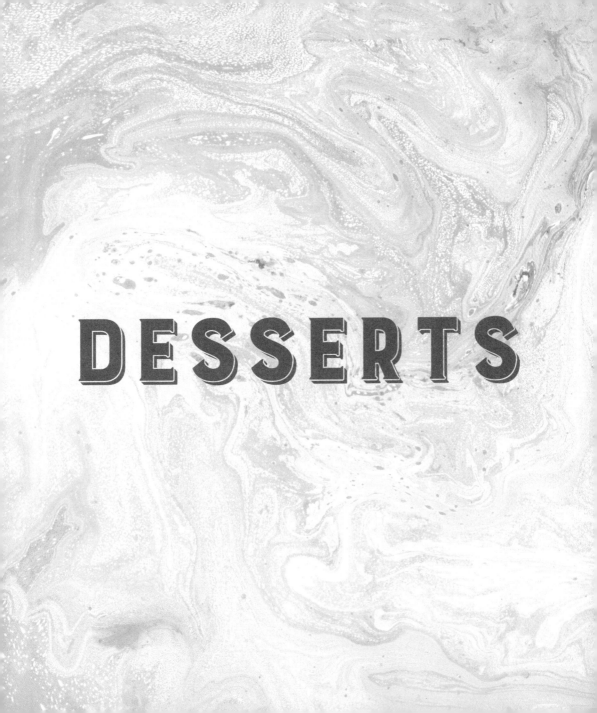

DESSERTS

✷ CHARMING CHEESECAKE ✷

No one can resist the charm of this magical rainbow cheesecake.

Makes: 6–8 servings ✷ Time: 1 hour 30 minutes, plus chilling time ✷
Difficulty rating: ⌒

INGREDIENTS

- ★ 400g pink wafer biscuits
- ★ 60g butter, melted
- ★ 3 tsp gelatine
- ★ 2 tbsp boiling water
- ★ 500g cream cheese
- ★ 80g sugar
- ★ 2 tsp vanilla extract
- ★ 300g double cream
- ★ Gel food colouring (pink, purple, blue and yellow)
- ★ Pink and purple sprinkles and edible glitter

EXTRA EQUIPMENT

You will need a 20cm springform tin and a food processor.

METHOD

To make the base, blitz the pink wafers in a food processor until they become fine crumbs. Pour the crumbs into a bowl and add the melted butter, mixing the two ingredients until they are fully combined. Next pour the mixture into the 20cm springform tin, pressing it down until compact then place in the fridge while you make the filling.

Pour the boiling water into a measuring jug and sprinkle the gelatine into the water, whisking it together with a fork while it dissolves.

Beat the cream cheese, vanilla extract and sugar into a large bowl until smooth and stir in the liquid gelatine. Whip the double cream until soft peaks form then fold into the cream cheese mixture and combine until smooth.

Divide the mixture evenly between four bowls and colour each to create four pastel-toned bowls of cheesecake mixture.

Take the chilled base out of the fridge and spoon the coloured cheesecake mixtures in a random formation on top of the pink wafer base. Smooth out the mixture and place the cheesecake back in the fridge to set for 2–3 hours.

Before serving, cover with a handful of sprinkles and glitter.

✴ PASTEL PAVLOVAS ✴

Unleash your inner unicorn with these cute mini pavlova desserts.

Makes: 4 pavlovas ✴ Time: 2 hours ✴ Difficulty rating: ◖◖

INGREDIENTS

- ★ 4 egg whites
- ★ 1 tsp cream of tartar
- ★ 220g caster sugar
- ★ Pink and blue gel food colouring
- ★ 200ml double cream
- ★ Handful fresh berries
- ★ Icing sugar to dust

EXTRA EQUIPMENT

You will need two piping bags and two round-tipped piping nozzles.

METHOD

Preheat the oven to 100ºC and line two baking trays with baking paper.

Place the egg whites and cream of tartar into a clean bowl and beat until soft peaks form. *NB: make sure no egg yolk infiltrates the egg white otherwise your meringue will fail.* Gradually add caster sugar 1 tbsp at a time, beating well in between each addition.

Continue beating until the mixture is thick and glossy then split it evenly between two bowls.

Add a few drops of pink gel food colouring to one bowl and a few drops of blue food gel colouring to the other, then transfer each mixture to a piping bag fitted with a round nozzle. Pipe eight blue meringues onto one of the lined baking trays and eight pink meringues onto the other. You will need two blue and two pink meringues for each pavlova.

Bake for 1 hour and leave to cool completely in the oven with the door ajar.

Whip the double cream until it thickens and begin layering your pavlova by adding 1 tbsp of the cream in between each meringue.

Top with a few fresh berries and a dusting of icing sugar and serve immediately.

✷ NEAPOLITAN MOUSSE ✷

Is there a happier more indulgent dessert combination than this light and fluffy mousse triplet?

Makes: 4 servings ✶ Time: 3 hours ✶ Difficulty rating: ◠ ◠

INGREDIENTS

* ★ 125g frozen raspberries
* ★ 60ml boiling water
* ★ 3 tsp gelatine
* ★ 560ml double cream
* ★ 4 egg yolks
* ★ 50g caster sugar
* ★ 250ml milk
* ★ 100g dark chocolate, finely chopped
* ★ 100g white chocolate, finely chopped
* ★ Handful fresh raspberries
* ★ 1 sprig of mint

EXTRA EQUIPMENT

You will need four serving glasses.

METHOD

Place the raspberries in a saucepan over a low heat and simmer for 5 minutes or until the raspberries collapse. Strain through a fine sieve into a bowl, using the back of a spoon to push as much pulp through as possible.

Place the boiling water in a small bowl and add the gelatine. Stir until the gelatine has fully dissolved then leave to one side.

Pour the cream into a large bowl and whisk until soft peaks form, cover with cling film and leave in the fridge or keep to one side.

Use a whisk or an electric handheld whisk to beat the egg yolks and sugar in a bowl until pale and creamy. Place the milk in a saucepan over a medium to high heat and bring it to a simmer. Gradually add it to the egg and sugar mix with the whisk on a low speed. Once fully combined, return to the saucepan and stir over a low heat for 5 minutes or until the mixture thickens and coats the back of a spoon. Remove the mixture from the heat, add the gelatine and stir until fully combined. You now have the base mix for your mousse. You'll have to work quickly for the next bit to make sure the base mix stays warm enough to melt your chocolate ingredients.

For the dark chocolate layer:

Place the finely chopped dark chocolate in a heatproof bowl and pour one-third of the base mix over it, stirring it until the chocolate melts and is smooth.

For the pink layer:

Pour in half of the remaining base mix over the raspberry puree and stir until combined.

For the white chocolate layer:

Place the white chocolate in a heatproof bowl and pour the remaining base mix over the top, stirring it until the chocolate has melted and is smooth.

To assemble your mousse:

Add a third of the cream into the chocolate mixture and gently fold it in to combine. Divide equally into your four serving dishes, cover each with cling film and leave in the fridge for 30 minutes or until just set.

Add half the remaining cream to the raspberry mixture and fold through to combine. Bring the set chocolate mousse out of the fridge and divide the raspberry mousse equally over the chocolate mousse. Cover again with cling film and return to the fridge to set for another 30 minutes.

Repeat with the remaining cream and white chocolate mixture and leave the layered mousse in the fridge for 2 hours or until completely set.

Serve with whipped cream and some fresh raspberries and mint to garnish.

✷ ENCHANTED ICE CREAM ✷

Guaranteed to make you smile, this enchanting no-churn vanilla rainbow ice cream is full of fun and flavour – the perfect way to cool down on a hot summer's day.

Makes: 6 servings ✳ Time: 30 minutes, plus overnight freezing ✳
Difficulty rating: �︵

INGREDIENTS

- ★ 800ml double cream
- ★ 2 tbsp vanilla extract
- ★ 1 can sweetened condensed milk
- ★ Gel food colouring (pink, purple, blue, yellow)
- ★ Unicorn Sprinkles (see page 93)

EXTRA EQUIPMENT

You will need a 23cm x 13cm loaf tin and an ice cream scoop.

METHOD

In a large bowl or a stand mixer, whip double cream and vanilla together for a few minutes until stiff peaks form.

Add in the sweetened condensed milk and whisk until combined.

Separate the mixture into four bowls.

Colour one bowl of the mixture with a few drops of the pink gel food colouring and combine well, adding more if desired.

Repeat with the remaining bowls of mixture and colours until you have one pink, one purple, one blue and one yellow.

Spoon the mixtures into the 23cm x 13cm loaf tin, alternating different spoonfuls of colour at a time.

Once all of the mixture is in the loaf tin, take a knife and run it through the mixture a few times gently swirling the colours together.

Scatter Unicorn Sprinkles over the top and freeze for several hours or overnight until set.

✶ TWINKLE TARTS ✶

These rich, dark and silky chocolate tarts encased in purple pastry will take you to dessert heaven.

Makes: 4 mini tarts   ✶   Time: 1 hour, plus chilling time   ✶
Difficulty rating: ◠ ◠

INGREDIENTS

For the pastry:

- ★ 300g flour
- ★ 150g butter, cold and cut into chunks
- ★ Purple gel food colouring
- ★ 75g ice cold water

For the ganache:

- ★ 200g double cream
- ★ 300g milk chocolate, chopped into small chunks

For the decoration:

- ★ 100g white chocolate to make curls
- ★ White pearl sprinkles
- ★ Silver edible glitter

EXTRA EQUIPMENT

You will need four 10cm tart tins, a rolling pin, ceramic baking beans and a vegetable peeler.

METHOD

For the pastry:

Before getting started please note that you will be kneading vibrant purple food colouring into this pastry using your hands so you may wish to wear some plastic gloves to avoid turning them purple.

To make the pastry, tip the flour into a large bowl and add the cold chunks of butter. Add 3–4 drops of the purple gel food colouring and rub everything together with your fingers until your mixture looks like breadcrumbs.

Measure out the water, add a few drops of purple colouring and mix it in. Add three-quarters of the water to the flour and bring the two mixtures together to form a rich, purple-coloured dough.

Flatten the dough, then wrap it tightly with cling film and chill in the fridge for 30 minutes or longer if you have time to spare.

Preheat the oven to 180°C and grease your four 10cm tart tins with plenty of butter.

Roll out your chilled pastry on a floured surface to approximately 3mm thickness. Cut into four squares and roll each one over the

mini tart tin, pushing it down against the sides. Trim the edges and leave at least 1cm overhang as it will shrink during baking.

Prick the base with a fork and line the pastry case with a square of baking paper and some ceramic baking beans. Bake for 15 minutes, remove the paper and bake for a further 10 minutes. Leave to cool while you make the ganache.

For the ganache:

Pour the cream into a small saucepan and bring to the boil. Remove from the heat and add the chopped milk chocolate. Leave for 2–3 minutes then gently mix the two together until the chocolate is completely melted and the ingredients are fully combined.

Transfer the ganache into a jug and pour it into each of the tart cases. Sprinkle them with edible glitter then place in the fridge to chill for 3 hours until set.

Bring the tarts to room temperature and top with some white chocolate curls made by running the blade of a vegetable peeler lengthways across a room-temperature bar of white chocolate. You can make these in advance if you wish and refrigerate the curls until ready to use.

Serve with a scattering of the white chocolate curls, a handful of white pearl sprinkles and a splash of cream.

DRINKS

✷ DREAMY HOT CHOCOLATE ✷

This smooth and creamy white hot chocolate will make all your dreams come true – you can't help but smile while you are drinking it.

Makes: 4 glasses ✳ **Time: 15 minutes** ✳ **Difficulty rating:** 🌈

INGREDIENTS

* ★ 700ml semi-skimmed milk
* ★ 1 tbsp vanilla extract
* ★ 200g white chocolate, chopped into small pieces
* ★ Pink gel food colouring
* ★ Unicorn Sprinkles (see page 93)

EXTRA EQUIPMENT

You will need four tall hot chocolate glasses or mugs.

METHOD

Place the milk, vanilla and chopped white chocolate in a medium saucepan and simmer on a medium heat, stirring occasionally with a whisk, until the white chocolate has melted.

Add 1 drop of pink food colouring just before the mixture comes to the boil and whisk it in, then as it begins to boil remove the pan from the heat and serve immediately.

Top with whipped cream, marshmallows and Unicorn Sprinkles if desired.

✷ STRAWBERRIES AND CREAM MILKSHAKE ✷

This indulgent sweet masterpiece is one seriously special treat. Let your creativity run wild and serve this chilled drink with a generous dollop of whipped cream and sprinkles, obviously.

Makes: Serves 2 ✷ **Time: 15 minutes** ✷ **Difficulty rating:** 🌙

INGREDIENTS

- ★ 2 tbsp melted white chocolate
- ★ 6 scoops vanilla ice cream
- ★ 10 chopped strawberries
- ★ 200ml semi-skimmed milk
- ★ Whipped cream from a can
- ★ Hundreds and thousands

EXTRA EQUIPMENT

You will need a blender and two glasses.

METHOD

Place the white chocolate in a bowl set over a pan of simmering water and melt until smooth. Prepare each glass by dipping the rim in the melted chocolate and coating it with sprinkles.

Put the vanilla ice cream, strawberries and milk in a blender and blitz until smooth.

Pour into your prepared glass and top with a generous dose of squirty cream and, yes, you guessed it, more sprinkles.

Serve immediately with a straw.

✷ RAINBOW SMOOTHIE ✷

Ever wondered what rainbows taste like? Well now you can find out with this colourful smoothie, which is fun to make and absolutely delicious to drink.

Makes: 2 glasses ✶ **Time: 15 minutes** ✶ **Difficulty rating:** 🌈

INGREDIENTS

For the yellow/orange layer:

- ★ 200g fresh mango
- ★ ½ banana
- ★ 50ml orange juice

For the purple layer:

- ★ 200g mixed berries
- ★ ½ banana
- ★ 2 tbsp honey

For the red layer:

- ★ 50g raspberries
- ★ 2 ice cubes

EXTRA EQUIPMENT

You will need a blender and two glasses.

METHOD

Using a blender, mix the ingredients for each layer separately, rinsing the blender in between layers, and pour the mixtures into separate bowls.

To layer the smoothie, start by carefully pouring a small amount of the yellow/orange layer to the bottom of the glass. Follow with a tablespoon of the purple layer then tip the glass at an angle and add another layer of yellow followed by a tablespoon of the red layer.

Finish with a generous final layer of purple until the glass is full and serve with a straw.

✦ UNICORN TEARS MOCKTAIL ✦

Yes, it's true that even unicorns cry sometimes. But their tears are filled with magical properties that heal and make you stronger (so lap up those tears and feel on top of the world).

Makes: 2 glasses   ✦   Time: 15 minutes   ✦   Difficulty rating: 🌈

INGREDIENTS

* ★ 3 tbsp sugar
* ★ 100ml cranberry juice
* ★ 20ml lime juice
* ★ Juice of 1 orange
* ★ 100ml soda water
* ★ 1 tbsp sprinkles for garnish

EXTRA EQUIPMENT

You will need a cocktail shaker, a shot measurer (a jigger) and two Martini glasses.

METHOD

In a small pan combine 2 tbsp sugar with 2 tbsp water. Heat until the water evaporates and you're left with a sugar syrup. Leave to one side.

Mix the remaining sugar and sprinkles together on a plate until well distributed.

Dip the rim of a cocktail glass into the sugar syrup, then dip this into the sugar and sprinkle mixture so the rim is coated.

In a shaker filled with ice, mix the cranberry juice, orange juice and lime juice.

Add the soda water and stir. Strain into the two prepared Martini glasses.

✶ INTERGALACTIC ICE CUBES ✶

These glitter bombs turn any ordinary drink into an extraordinary, celestial experience.

Makes: 12 ice cubes ✶ Time: 10 minutes, plus freezing ✶
Difficulty rating: ◠

INGREDIENTS

- ★ 400ml water
- ★ Assorted purple sprinkles
- ★ Edible glitter, purple and silver

EXTRA EQUIPMENT

You will need an ice cube tray.

METHOD

Fill the bottom of an ice cube tray with an assortment of purple sprinkles.

Pour water into each hole and fill to the top. Freeze until set.

Remove from the freezer and brush the tops with a mixture of purple and silver edible glitter.

Place in the fridge for 20 minutes so the glitter can bind to the ice and serve as you need.

400ML water
Assorted
Edible glitter

INDEX